Available From the American Academy of Pediatrics

Achieving a Healthy Weight for Your Child: An Action Plan for Families

ADHD: What Every Parent Needs to Know

Allergies and Asthma: What Every Parent Needs to Know

Autism Spectrum Disorder: What Every Parent Needs to Know

Baby and Toddler Basics: Expert Answers to Parents' Top 150 Questions

The Big Book of Symptoms: A–Z Guide to Your Child's Health

Building Resilience in Children and Teens: Giving Kids Roots and Wings

Caring for Your Adopted Child: An Essential Guide for Parents

Caring for Your Baby and Young Child: Birth to Age 5*

Caring for Your School-Age Child: Ages 5–12

Dad to Dad: Parenting Like a Pro

Food Fights: Winning the Nutritional Challenges of Parenthood Armed
With Insight, Humor, and a Bottle of Ketchup

Guide to Toilet Training

Heading Home With Your Newborn: From Birth to Reality

Mama Doc Medicine: Finding Calm and Confidence in Parenting,
Child Health, and Work-Life Balance

My Child Is Sick! Expert Advice for Managing Common Illnesses and Injuries

Nutrition: What Every Parent Needs to Know

Parenting Through Puberty: Mood Swings, Acne, and Growing Pains

The Picky Eater Project: 6 Weeks to Happier, Healthier Family Mealtimes

Raising Kids to Thrive: Balancing Love With Expectations and Protection With Trust

Retro Baby: Cut Back on All the Gear and Boost Your Baby's Development With More
Than 100 Time-tested Activities

Retro Toddler: More Than 100 Old-School Activities to Boost Development

Sleep: What Every Parent Needs to Know

Waking Up Dry: A Guide to Help Children Overcome Bedwetting

Your Baby's First Year*

*This book is also available in Spanish.

**For additional parenting resources, visit the HealthyChildren bookstore at
https://shop.aap.org/for-parents.**

healthychildren.org
Powered by pediatricians. Trusted by parents.
from the American Academy of Pediatrics

Raising an Organized Child

5 Steps to
- ☑ Boost Independence
- ☑ Ease Frustration
- ☑ Promote Confidence

Damon Korb, MD, FAAP

American Academy of Pediatrics

DEDICATED TO THE HEALTH OF ALL CHILDREN®

American Academy of Pediatrics Publishing Staff

Mary Lou White, *Chief Product and Services Officer/SVP, Membership, Marketing, and Publishing*
Mark Grimes, *Vice President, Publishing*
Holly Kaminski, Editor, Consumer Publishing
Shannan Martin, *Production Manager, Consumer Publications*
Amanda Helmholz, *Medical Copy Editor*
Sara Hoerdeman, *Marketing Manager, Consumer Products*

Published by the American Academy of Pediatrics
345 Park Blvd
Itasca, IL 60143
Telephone: 630/626-6000
Facsimile: 847/434-8000
www.aap.org

The American Academy of Pediatrics is an organization of 67,000 primary care pediatricians, pediatric medical subspecialists, and pediatric surgical specialists dedicated to the health, safety, and well-being of infants, children, adolescents, and young adults.

The information contained in this publication should not be used as a substitute for the medical care and advice of your pediatrician. There may be variations in treatment that your pediatrician may recommend based on individual facts and circumstances.

Statements and opinions expressed are those of the authors and not necessarily those of the American Academy of Pediatrics.

Listing of resources does not imply an endorsement by the American Academy of Pediatrics (AAP). The AAP is not responsible for the content of external resources. Information was current at the time of publication.

Products and Web sites are mentioned for informational purposes only and do not imply an endorsement by the American Academy of Pediatrics. Web site addresses are as current as possible but may change at any time.

Brand names are furnished for identification purposes only. No endorsement of the manufacturers or products mentioned is implied.

The publishers have made every effort to trace the copyright holders for borrowed materials. If they have inadvertently overlooked any, they will be pleased to make the necessary arrangements at the first opportunity.

This publication has been developed by the American Academy of Pediatrics. The contributors are expert authorities in the field of pediatrics. No commercial involvement of any kind has been solicited or accepted in development of the content of this publication. There are no disclosures.

Every effort is made to keep *Raising an Organized Child* consistent with the most recent advice and information available from the American Academy of Pediatrics.

Special discounts are available for bulk purchases of this publication. E-mail Special Sales at aapsales@aap.org for more information.

Printed in the United States of America
9-412   1 2 3 4 5 6 7 8 9 10
CB0112
ISBN: 978-1-61002-282-8
eBook: 978-1-61002-283-5
EPUB: 978-1-61002-284-2
Kindle: 978-1-61002-285-9
PDF: 978-1-61002-286-6

Cover design by Daniel Rembert
Back cover photograph by Stephanie Waisler Rubin
Publication design by R. Scott Rattray
Original artwork by Tatum Elyse Korb. Reproduced with permission.
Library of Congress Control Number: 2018946356

What People Are Saying

If your family has experienced lost homework, or a misplaced shoe, or your child's bedroom looks like a tornado hit it, then this book is for you! Dr Korb's advice will help parents reduce day-to-day frustrations with homework, routines, clutter, and more. But, more importantly, Dr Korb's guidance on boosting children's organizational skills and executive function will prepare today's toddlers and teens for success as adults."

—Tanya Altmann, MD, FAAP, author of *Baby and Toddler Basics* and mom of 3 boys

Parenting a child with ADHD or other attentional and learning problems can be stressful. As a behavioral pediatrician who specializes in ADHD and parenting, I look forward to recommending this book to my patients, their families, and the readers of my blog! It offers readers concrete, practical, and well-described strategies parents can begin using right away. The 5 steps are repeated depending on the age of your child, which means you don't have to read the book cover to cover but instead reach for it time and again! This book fills a gap in the parenting literature out there for supporting children with attentional difficulties. Thank you, Dr Korb!

—Nerissa S. Bauer, MD, MPH, FAAP, behavioral pediatrician and blogger at Let's Talk Kids Health

Dr Korb is to be commended for focusing parents' attention on their children's organizational capabilities as key components of success. His book is itself a model of organization, with (as Dr Korb would say) everything in its place. It's fascinating to see how the 5 principles of organization apply at each stage of development. Speaking personally, as one who only recently learned how not to lose his car keys on a weekly basis, this is a book that might have helped me growing up!

—**Robert Needlman, MD, coauthor of** *Dr. Spock's Baby and Child Care* **and professor of pediatrics, Case Western Reserve University School of Medicine**

I'll share this book with so many of my clients. Dr Korb describes a compelling approach, grounded in research, for developing internal organization by strategically structuring a child's external surroundings. This book will help parents and educators of young children prevent disorganization while also illuminating the path for older students to overcome organization challenges. Organization is critically important, and Dr Korb gives hope for achieving it.

—**Craig Pohlman, PhD, author of** *Revealing Minds* **and** *How Can My Kid Succeed in School?* **and chief executive officer, Southeast Psych**

Parents who are highly organized at home, at work, and in their social interactions and parents who find an organized life to be a challenge share a desire to raise their children to appreciate the value of planning and organizing. Dr Korb encourages parents to teach their children principles of organization as a guiding theme to understand and nurture emotional, social, and cognitive development. Each stage of development is discussed in the context of the wide range of normal maturation. Parents will find guides to recognize behavioral cues and utilize effective strategies to enhance organized behavior and thinking. An added benefit of the book is the numerous discussions about the neurological maturation of the human brain and its effect on a child's emotional life and learning.

—**Martin T. Stein, MD, professor emeritus of pediatrics, University of California San Diego, Rady Children's Hospital**

Contents

Acknowledgments

The creation of *Raising an Organized Child* has been a labor of love. The writing of it was tucked into the few precious moments when I was not spending time with the family I love or performing the work I love. A plane ride here, a late night there. On the sidelines of a soccer practice and the bleachers of a gymnasium.

Thank you to the American Academy of Pediatrics (AAP) for publishing this guidebook for parents. It has been a pleasure to work with everyone in AAP Publishing. Special thanks to my editor, Holly Kaminski, who not only helped clarify my message but, as a mom, recognized the value in this book.

While writing *Raising an Organized Child,* I stood on the broad shoulders of many educators, psychologists, and physicians who have researched learning, executive functions, and development. I recognize their contributions to this book and the greater scientific understanding of child development.

Along my journey, I have had wonderful mentors. My parents, David and Darlene Korb, who were brave enough to let me solve problems on my own. Thank you to Joseph Kertes, PhD, for taking me down the path of psychobiology. My gratitude goes out to Brenda Lee, MEd, who mentored me through medical school. Thank you to Stu Teplin, MD; Lynn Wegner, MD; and Bill Coleman, MD, for setting me on a wonderful path toward developmental and behavioral pediatrics. Thank you to Brad Berman, MD, and Michelle Macias, MD, for their mentorship along the way and for their careful review of this book. And a warm appreciation to Christopher Greeley, MD, and Nerissa Bauer, MD, who also took the time to review and improve this manuscript.

I have tremendous gratitude for my supportive family. I am inspired by 5 magnificent children, Kevin, Cameron, Cassie, Tatum, and Alexis. I have learned more about being a pediatrician from you than you could imagine. Thanks to you all, I can honestly turn to my patients and say, "I understand," because I know how much a parent can love a child. Thank you for letting me coach your teams, take you on camping trips, and watch you grow up. Your adventures make me proud. Thank you for letting me share your stories in this book. Hopefully, your stories will help many families *raise organized kids* like you.

To my wife, Amy; my admiration for you has grown each of the 25 years that we have been married. I have learned so many lessons from you. You were an editor and a powerful guide for this book. You are truly the most organized person who I have ever met. When filing cabinets were not large enough, they invented computers to store the mountains of information that you somehow keep organized in your mind. You have taught me to be a "closer."

Finally, thank you to my wonderful patients and their passionate parents. We learn from each other. This book is a gift from you and to you.

Introduction

A Parent's Predicament in Supporting a Growing Child's Organization

Organized thinking is defined much more broadly than neatness. A messy room and crumpled papers in a backpack will only scratch the surface of organized thinking. Think of the most organized person who you have ever met. Certainly, his or her house is likely kept orderly, but the most impressive thing about organized people is how they think. They have a tremendous sense of the big picture that allows them to effectively and confidently make decisions and budget their time. These people always seem to be thinking 2 steps ahead. Now, what does being organized look like in children? Well, they may be more prepared and independent than, and less likely to get caught up in "the drama" with, their peers. Yet the opposite is true for a child who has problems showing insight, anticipating, or grasping the big picture.

Raising a disorganized child is particularly frustrating for parents, because a child's struggles are often both inconsistent and difficult to define. Tasks that seem second nature or common sense to parents, such as turning in a completed homework assignment, finding one's shoes, or getting ready for bed, become insurmountable obstacles for a disorganized child; despite scores of reminders and demonstrations, the miscues continue. Parents become frustrated by their child's repeated struggles to take ownership of daily routines. They want to know why their child cannot complete tasks. As a disorganized child gets older and enters school, parents may become acutely aware of, and preoccupied with, all their child's difficulties—sometimes overlooking their child's many strengths. Parents may begin to feel guilty and then wonder whether they enabled their child's disorganization by doing too much work for her. They question whether they will be dressing, feeding, and doing homework with their child even when she is a young adult. How can they enable their child to develop into a competent individual when they feel compelled to support most everything she does?

As a developmental and behavioral pediatrician, I have been offered the unique opportunity to care for thousands of young individuals who struggle at school for a variety of reasons, such as variation in neurodevelopment (when the nervous system, which controls how we think, move, learn, and behave, develops differently than expected), cognitive deficits (intellectual ability that is far below average), language delays, attention dysfunctions (problems with focus, concentration, and self-control), and emotional issues. Some of these children carry a diagnosis such as autism spectrum disorder, attention-deficit/hyperactivity disorder, learning disabilities, obsessive-compulsive disorder, fetal alcohol syndrome, anxiety, or quite often a combination of these conditions.

Families share with me how each of their lives are affected by these circumstances: the hours of homework, the pain of watching their child struggle, and not to mention how the financial and time drains of multiple therapies take a toll on a family. For some, the effect is unbearable; it has been reported that when a family has a child with special needs, 80% of these families' marriages end in a divorce.[1-3] Having a child struggle is serious business.

Often it is the fear of the unknown that puts stress onto the family. Parents ask me, "What will my child be like when he is an adult?"

Sometimes, very tongue-in-cheek, they ask, "Will my son ever move out of the house?" I think that when they ask me this latter question, they are only half joking, because progress is slow and the unknown future for a child who struggles can be terrifying to a parent.

A child need not have a severe disability for it to create stress in the family. Most children struggle in one way or another because of subtle variations in their neurodevelopmental abilities. Misunderstood weakness in memory, attention, organizing, or social cognition (how people understand and apply information about other people during daily interactions) can wreak havoc on a child's social or academic status. These issues can often be addressed through accommodations and treatments, once the problem is clearly identified.

Fortunately, for most of the children I serve, a relatively clear, although often arduous, treatment plan exists. I call these plans Developing Minds Action Plans. For example, a child with dyslexia can find success with months, to years, of an intensive, multisensory reading program. When a clear treatment plan is available to families, I witness the empowerment they feel as they set out to support their child. In the absence of a clear plan, families appear overwhelmed by the prospect of supporting their struggling child. Often, they turn to unproven therapies, sometimes spending thousands of dollars, searching for solutions, adding financial stress to an already difficult situation. Raising a disorganized child is particularly frustrating for parents, because a child's struggles can be pervasive, inconsistent, and difficult to define.

Having worked with children for decades, I can say with confidence that most organized children do not suddenly appear—they are raised. The brain functions required for organization start forming shortly after birth. When nurtured, children grow up empowered by their independence. Each child takes a unique developmental path; some brains develop earlier and some later. Some children, such as those with attention-deficit/hyperactivity disorder or a learning disability, develop differently, making tasks such as organization more difficult. The key to supporting children is to meet them at their level of development and gradually push them forward by challenging them to learn new skills. Tasks in life become increasingly complicated as children grow older, and brain development in the ability to remember and understand organization is required to keep up with these demands.

The Purpose of This Book

The purpose of *Raising an Organized Child* is to provide a guide for parents on how to raise an independent, self-assured, and organized child. Doing so will boost your child's independence, ease frustration, and promote confidence. The information is intended to help parents understand the struggles of their disorganized child, thereby minimizing parental frustration, and subsequent misunderstanding, through understanding and support.

This book gives an overview of early brain development as it relates to organization and provides appropriate age-based milestones for organizational skills. The neurodevelopmental functions that contribute to organization are described. You will be shown how dysfunctions (breakdowns or lacks) in these neurodevelopmental systems can interfere with a child's everyday activities. Most important, the book provides practical solutions for parents and teachers to help children develop their organizational abilities.

- New parents of young children can use this book to immunize their child against future organizational struggles.
- Parents who are already strongly affected by their child's disorganization will be empowered to create an individualized treatment plan that consists of strategies for improving their child's organizational skills.
- Finally, teachers can provide families with valuable tips and recommendations to address a student's organizational deficits in the classroom. Remember, organized children are not born—they are raised.

Why This Book Is Important

A growing body of research from the fields of psychology, neuropsychology, and medicine describes how the brain supports organized thinking, and numerous books exist that provide parents and students with organizational strategies to assist with tasks at school and at home. But there have not been books that define the neurodevelopmental abilities that are critical for organization and then show parents how to develop their child's organized thinking skills. This book shows parents how to teach their children to use organized thinking to show insight, plan ahead, and grasp the big picture.

Raising an Organized Child should empower you, as a parent, to support your emerging organized child at levels that are developmentally appropriate. This book spans infancy through the teen years so that you can refer back to this book as your child grows older. Use the milestones in this book to understand how hard to push your child, and use the interventions to support your child if he starts falling behind. You might even learn a little bit about how your organized brain works, and the realization that we all think differently and we all have strengths and weaknesses helps us understand that every child follows a unique and special path.

Using This Book

I believe that the best way to prepare your child's brain for adulthood is to teach him to be an organized thinker. Consider the proverb "Give a man a fish, and you feed him for a day. Teach a man to fish, and you feed him for a lifetime." Many parents fall into the trap of giving their young child new skills instead of strengthening his ability to think. Teaching a child to say the alphabet at age 2 years or to read by age 3 is like a cool party trick. These skills are fun to show off to your friends but, in reality, they do very little to prepare your child for later social and academic successes. Your efforts will be best spent helping your child become an organized thinker, because an organized thinker is better prepared to learn. An organized thinker can compare and contrast, consider numerous outcomes and possibilities, formulate his own opinion, create, and invent.

Adults (both within the home and outside the home) foster the development of executive functions (brain skills needed for planning, task completion, and self-regulation) in a child by showing confidence in the ability of the child and gradually encouraging the child to assume the "executive" role for herself. The trick is to support children with reasonable expectations that propel them forward at their own speed, but not too fast or too slow. Young children need greater supervision and scaffolding (a process during which solving a problem is modeled or demonstrated and then support is gradually stepped back) to organize the world around them, and as they get older, they need increasing opportunities to make decisions and mature.[4,5] It also seems that environments that are both more ordered and more predictable promote the development of executive functioning skills.[4,6] The most supportive environments share qualities including responsive caregiving, consistency, and protection from sustained stress.

Children are very different from each other. The height of each child is a perfect example of this because some children grow very early and others grow late. The same is true for cognitive growth (brain development). So get to know your child and support her at the appropriate developmental level. Some children have naturally stronger organizational skills and others need more support. Great parenting can overcome giant obstacles, and in the absence of good parenting, even the most talented child can struggle to behave, socialize, and learn in a productive manner. Whether a child masters the steps of being organized depends on the parent's ability to teach and actualize the child's organizational skills.

Organization of the Book

The content of *Raising an Organized Child* is arranged to correspond with a child's developmental level, so that parents can have a better understanding of their child's organizational skills level, thereby enabling them to provide the right amount of support.

Each of the upcoming chapters of this book addresses specific interventions to support your child's organizational progress. The interventions challenge children to exercise their executive functioning skills. My experience as a pediatrician and parent for more than 20 years has helped me understand that there are basic principles to follow when raising organized kids. This book puts the organizational expectations into a context of what is developmentally appropriate and explains the 5 Steps to Raising an Organized Child.

1. Be consistent.
2. Introduce order.
3. Give everything a place.
4. Practice forward thinking: planning, estimating, and creativity.
5. Promote problem-solving.

When children are very young, the first steps, starting with consistency, are most important. As children get older, the first steps remain important, but additional steps, such as introducing order and giving everything a place, increase in importance. Once a child is a preschooler, and her brain is beginning to understand concepts, the importance of forward thinking and problem-solving increases. After that, all these interventions are important, but the implementation and teaching of these steps varies by age.

These interventions are organized by age so that you can have a general understanding of when to expect a milestone. That said, your child may not be average. Your child may be advanced in one domain and delayed in the next, so it is important to promote growth according to your child's individual needs and not necessarily her chronological age. It does not help to set age-appropriate expectations if your child has organizational deficits. Start at her level and then, as she progresses, increase the demands placed onto her organizational skills.

My Organizational Experience

As a parent of 5 children and the husband of a remarkably organized wife, I have real-life experience raising organized children. In addition, I have coached more than 20 seasons of youth sports and my older children have gone on to play college sports. Coaching has allowed me to observe how organized thinking is displayed outside the classroom. What I have learned is that the same organized thinking skills are valuable in athletics, academics, and social relationships. I hope that the stories about my family, my patients, my work, and my coaching experiences that I share in *Raising an Organized Child* will give you, the reader, the understanding that all children struggle and that with patience and guidance they can grow up into happy and thriving adults.

This book, as a reminder, should empower you, as a parent, to support your emerging organized child at levels that are developmentally appropriate. This book spans infancy through the teen years so that you can refer back to this book as your child continues to grow older. Use the milestones in this book to understand how hard to push your child, and use the interventions to support your child if he starts falling behind. You might even learn a little bit about how your organized brain works, and the realization that we all think differently and we all have strengths and weaknesses helps us understand that every child follows a unique and special path.

Chapter 1

Child Development and Brain Organization

The concepts and recommendations described in *Raising an Organized Child* are directly or indirectly supported by years of scientific evidence about how the brain evolves with age and how organizational skills develop over time. This chapter focuses on the scientific discovery and fascinating process by which clinicians grew to understand the organized brain and provides background on the evidence that supports the practical teachings discussed in this book.

As a result, the material discussed in this chapter is a bit more technical in nature than the rest of the book. The material is being provided for any readers who wish to further their understanding of the scientific rationale for the importance of cultivating an organized mind. Because, as every parent knows, even your preschoolers will ask, "Why?" to most of your requests since even they know that the explanation is important. This chapter focuses on the "Why?" and the following chapters address the "How?" As such, this chapter is not necessarily critical or essential to your understanding of the practical advice and suggestions provided in subsequent chapters.

Organization of Cognitive Functions

Organized thinking covers more than just being messy or late. An organized child has not only the neurodevelopmental capacity (memory and thinking skills) to store and retrieve sequential and spatial observations and data (information about order, shape, and size), but the ability to process multiple layers of information simultaneously. The organized brain is capable of higher-order cognition, including conceptualizing, perspective taking, creativity, and complex decision-making. These mental tasks require a very complicated system of neurological integration (brain wiring that connects thought).

The brain relies on an intricate network of interconnected brain functions. The brain's organization is similar to the layout of a large city. Cities are divided into districts, such as industrial, residential, shopping, and entertainment. In a city, crisscrossing highways connect these districts and carry traffic back and forth.

The brain is similarly divided into regions of **neurodevelopmental function,** such as memory, language, spatial and sequential processing, and motor control. Skills that a student must perform, such as writing a name, remembering homework, and playing dodgeball, require communication between these brain districts, or **neurodevelopmental functions.** For instance, consider a simple skill such as getting dressed in the morning. This task requires the sensory and motor systems to work in unison because coordination and balance are needed to put on clothes; dressing requires memory, for example, to remember that underwear should be worn before the pants, and so the brain creates a "getting dressed plan" that is stored and accessed each morning; attention must be given to details such as zipping the zipper and remembering to tie shoes; and tying shoes requires an element of sequential processing, because a number of steps are needed to make a proper bow. So, to complete even simple tasks such as getting dressed, a child's brain must network a complicated series of functions that occur in different regions of the brain. When one looks at it that way, it is almost a miracle that children make it to school each day!

Nerves in the brain serve the same function as do roads in a crowded city. They create a channel for communication between brain centers. The neural network is much more complicated than the congested Los Angeles freeway system. In fact, there are trillions of brilliantly orchestrated nerve highways where information travels at unimaginably high speeds. These nerves allow for different brain functions to communicate. With so much traffic, traveling at such high speeds, one would think that traffic crashes would frequently occur. If "crashes" happened in the brain, which they do, what would that look like? Picture a child who raises his hand in class in response to a teacher's question, and then, when called on, he forgets what he wanted to say. Consider a student who cannot help blurting out answers when the teacher is talking or interrupts his parents when they are on the phone. Remember the child who emotionally falls apart when he does not have situations go his way. Another common mental crash occurs when children are unable to pull themselves away from the television set or computer in order to get ready for school in the morning. These crashes occur in all people, but they happen more frequently when a person's brain is insufficiently organized.

Neurodevelopment of the Brain

The intricacies of the human brain and how it functions are a never-ending adventure. Each new discovery leads to even more questions. Research over the past century has provided insight into how the brain supports organizational skills. We can now point to a few specific regions of the brain that work together to support organized thoughts and actions. Some discoveries have been serendipitous (helpful even though they were made by chance, when looking into something else), such as those that result from assessing unintentional brain injuries. More-recent advancements in our understanding of the brain have come from exciting new technologies, such as brain imaging scans. Brain imaging technology allows researchers not only to take pictures of parts of the brain but also to watch how blood flows inside the brain while patients perform different types of mental tasks. The understanding is that brain regions that are activated require blood to deliver more oxygen. Elements of the **executive functions (brain skills needed for planning, task completion, and self-regulation)** can be measured with specific pencil-and-paper and thinking tasks. This allows clinicians to observe planning and organizational functions in a clinician's office. By using these tools with people who struggle, and with those who have savant or gifted abilities, scientists continue to expand the collective understanding about the efficient functioning of the brain. These tools, when applied to children of different ages, help us create a set of developmental organizational milestones that parents can use to guide their children's intellectual and functional growth.

The Famous Case of Phineas Gage

The frontal lobe has been associated with the **executive functions** in the scientific literature since the famous case of Phineas Gage. Phineas Gage is the first well-documented person to have survived severe brain damage, and his subsequent change in personality and function led scientists to believe that certain brain functions can be localized in specific regions of the brain. Phineas Gage was the foreman of a railway construction gang. On September 13, 1848, he and his crew were using explosives to clear a path for the Rutland and Burlington Railroad in Vermont. As Gage was using a tamping iron to pack the gunpowder into a hole in the rock, a spark led to the unintentional explosion that blew the 3 ft 7 in (1 m) long and 1¼ in (3 cm) diameter-wide rod through his head. The tamping iron went in point first under his left cheek bone and completely out through the top of his head, landing about 25 to 30 yd (23–27 m) behind him. Gage was knocked over but may not have lost consciousness even though most of the front part of the left side of his brain was destroyed.

Miraculously, Gage survived, likely because of the heat of the explosion, which cauterized, or burned closed, the injured blood vessels, limiting bleeding. He was hospitalized for 10 weeks and then released to resume his life. Some 9 months later, Gage felt strong enough to resume work, but he had trouble finding a job. Before the injury, he was reported to have been a capable and efficient foreman, who was effective at both business and managing his team. After the injury, he was impatient, obstinate, fitful, and grossly profane. He was unable to settle on any of the plans he devised for future action. His friends said he was "no longer Gage."

Gage lived for another 11½ years after the injury. He never resumed his job as a foreman. He worked in stables in New Hampshire and Chile, and for a couple years he was a living exhibit at Barnum's American Museum in New York. He died in 1860, and 7 years later his body was exhumed for medical research. His skull and the tamping iron are now on display at the Harvard University Countway Library of Medicine and serve as symbols of an early discovery about brain function.

More recently, studies of patients who have brain injuries, particularly strokes, have helped scientists isolate brain function throughout the brain. A stroke occurs when blood supply to a portion of the brain is impaired; sometimes these incidents can affect very specific parts of the brain. When patients have a blockage, or a leakage, to a blood vessel in the prefrontal cortex (the front part of the brain responsible for executive function control), physicians can correlate daily life function with the specific location of the brain injury. Daily life function (eg, cooking, housekeeping, taking medication as prescribed) requires a significant amount of planning, and it tends to be compromised after certain types of cerebral vascular injuries (eg, stroke). The effects of brain injuries to the prefrontal cortex have been described in rehabilitation settings.[7] The Allen Cognitive Level Screen (ACLS)[8] rates performance on a variety of executive tasks, and scores correlate with performance on activities of daily living that require planning. Thus, with imaging technology and measures such as the ACLS, scientists have been able to map specific regions of the brain with performance on pencil-and-paper and thinking tasks and with daily life function.

Scientists have imaging studies that allow us to take live pictures of the thinking brain. These technologies allow scientists to track the flow of oxygenated blood through the brain's blood vessels while children think (eg, perform math or solve puzzles), and this allows them to postulate where, in the brain, different types of thinking take place. Also, **quantitative electroencephalographs** are used to track the brain's electricity during brain work as axons in the brain carry electrical messages to stimulate thought. The precision of this testing begs the question, why not just do a brain imaging study of every child to see whether the child might have attention-deficit/hyperactivity disorder, autism spectrum disorder, or some other condition?

The answer to this question is complicated. Aside from the small medical risk that accompanies certain medical tests, the fact is that at the time this book was published, the data suggest that these tests, in most cases, are not any more accurate in finding a diagnosis than an interview by a good clinician. The difficulty in making a diagnosis stems from the fact that each brain is unique in its wiring and connections. It would be easy to make a diagnosis if brains were identical and imaging could detect a clump of nerves that were out of place, but the reality is that each brain has its own architecture.

One way to explain the variability in brains is to describe a scatterplot. A simple example might be estimating the sex of a person by plotting the length of his or her hair. Most of the girls would be on the long hair side of the scatterplot, and most of the boys would be on the short hair side, but there would be plenty of girls with short hair and many boys with longer hair than most girls. Therefore, the length of an individual's hair can be used only as an estimate of a person's sex. Similarly, a SPECT scan or an electroencephalogram, at this time, can offer only an estimate of the origin of a person's behavior using the typical wiring pattern of a brain.

We know from studies of brain injury in young children that one must use the word *typical* carefully when describing brain wiring since brains are plastic. *Plasticity* refers to the capacity of a brain to change or adapt. When a child, for instance, has a stroke that affects his ability to move his arm, through physical therapy the brain can recruit new pathways to control that function. Since the brain is capable of structural change when challenged, at this point it is difficult to rely on a computerized technology that is based on an average or typical presentation to make a diagnosis. Still, technology studies form an important avenue for future research and discovery. Your pediatrician should be able to advise you on the pros and cons of new diagnostic techniques.

Executive Functions

The organizational brain functions occur most notably in the prefrontal lobe, a section of the brain located about 2 in (5 cm) from the front and top of the brain. This organization center of the brain, commonly referred to as the **"executive function center,"** commands self-control, sequential and spatial organization processing, shifting thoughts, and simultaneous processing. **Sequential processing** describes order and timing. **Spatial processing** covers location. **Shifting** allows the brain to smoothly flex from one thought to the next. But the concept of simultaneous processing is more complicated.

Simultaneous processing refers to the brain's ability to think about more than one thing at a time. It is also sometimes referred to as the *working memory* of the brain. Consider the working memory as a mental whiteboard that holds on to multiple pieces of information at a time. For example, on a whiteboard it is much easier to write out a math calculation than to remember the steps in one's head. Likewise, when dialing a phone number, one might forget the number during the act of dialing unless she writes it down. When the working memory is intact, the brain can manage multiple simultaneous thoughts.

So how does this apply to organization? Well, most organized thought can be traced through the working memory center of the brain. It is like the Grand Central Terminal for organization in the brain. Planning involves the working memory, because it allows a child to think about multiple steps at a time. The working memory is also involved in taking perspective. For instance, when a child shares with a friend, that child is not only thinking about his desires but also using his mental whiteboard to consider the perspective of his playmate. The working memory helps children make choices, because the mental whiteboard works like a drop-down menu of options.

Younger children have less control of their working memory and therefore demonstrate more disorganized thinking. Quite often, young, and some older, disorganized thinkers react to new situations in only one ineffective manner, sometimes referred to as *reflexive negativity.* One mother of a patient said that her son's first response is always no, regardless of what she asks him to do. Whether she remarks, "Please take out the trash" or "Let's go to a movie," his first response is to say no. It does not matter how much he may enjoy going to movies—even if the movie is about his favorite thing—he always says no. Quite often, reflexively negative kids have faulty "drop-down menus." The drop-down menus of the brain are analogous to how computers are organized. When an organized child is confronted with a dilemma such as free time, he should have access to a metaphorical mental drop-down menu of options. But when this menu does not spontaneously appear, a disorganized child chooses to respond with the first action that pops into his mind, which these days is often a computer game or social media. Reflexive negativity is commonly observed in 2-year-olds, because 2-year-olds are by definition disorganized. Their response is usually no. When this behavior continues beyond the age of 5 years, it is problematic and should be discussed with your child's pediatrician.

Sometimes when kids get older, a lack of a functional, instantaneous drop-down menu system is associated with boredom. Children often appear bored, because they cannot consider a mental list of activities to do.

The **cognitive executive functions,** including simultaneous process-ing, sequential and spatial processing, and cognitive shifting, allow for the following complicated organizational thought and more:

- Remembering order
- Planning ahead
- Flexible thinking (considering and creating multiple responses or behavior options)
- Demonstrating insight or grasping the big picture
- Locating possessions
- Transitioning smoothly from one task to the next
- Coordinating movements while participating in a sport (a motor plan)
- Communicating effectively
- Taking perspective

These organizational skills become increasingly important as children grow into young adults, and fortunately, brain development usually meets the increasing demands. Because the demands change, students who may perform adeptly at one level can suddenly struggle at the next. We often see this in middle school students who excel through elementary school but are not ready for the organizational expectations of middle school. When discussing organization in children, it is important to describe not only the roles of organization but also the developmental expectations. The later chapters of this book demonstrate the expected development of organizational skills by age, but when reading forward, remember that by age 5 years, there is already a tremendous variability among children in their organizational skills. Therefore, the best way to use this book is to identify the level of your child and use the strategies for that age to propel her forward.

Development of Organizational Skills

As children grow, so do their organizational skills, yet each child progresses at his or her own rate. This section highlights some of the research that demonstrates how organizational capabilities grow with age. Early signs of **executive functioning** are evident before a child turns 1 year. A toddler can follow a brief plan or make simple decisions using one piece of available information. Three-year-olds can complete tasks that require them to make a decision between 2 separate rules. They demonstrate the flexibility to make choices and maintain focus despite the distractions of performing a task. By the time children enter preschool, they are often capable of following a group plan. They can execute plans independently when cued by subtle signs made by the classroom teacher and can ignore distractions for 15 to 20 minutes while they participate in circle time.

The A Not B Task

Many studies have demonstrated the growth of executive functions during the first years after birth. A pioneer in child development, Jean Piaget,[9] performed an experiment called the A Not B Task with young children aged 7 months and older. In this experiment, the children are shown an eye-catching toy. The toy is placed into Box A, within the child's reach, and the child is allowed to search for the toy. This action is repeated several times. Then, while the child is still watching, the toy is placed into Box B, also within the child's reach. What Piaget found is that children younger than 12 months consistently went to Box A to find the missing object. The theory is that the introduction of the second box was too much for them to consider. It overwhelmed their processing. Unable to focus on more than one thing at a time, the children perseverated on the 1 box that had become familiar to them, Box A. Children closer to age 12 months were not distracted by the rehearsals and were able to consider other possibilities (Box B).

Other researchers have since made the A Not B Task more complicated by hiding the attractive toy in a box that requires several steps to access and challenges older children.[10] Just like in the Piaget experiment, the children are allowed to access the toy in Box A over several trials and then, as the child watches, the toy is placed into Box B, which also requires several steps to access. What was found is interesting: the 12- to 24-month-old toddlers who could easily perform the Piaget experiment reverted in this experiment to choosing Box A, and many would choose Box A repeatedly over multiple challenges. The children's working memory was exhausted by the multiple-step box and prevented them from solving the problem. Too much memory was required. During the third year after birth, children begin to develop the problem-solving skills needed to complete this task.

Following Rules

In an experiment related to the A Not B Task, David Zelazo, PhD, tested 2-, 3-, and 4-year-olds' abilities to follow rules. In the Dimensional Card Sort Task, children were given cards with 2 sets of pictures (cars and flowers) and each of these pictures could be one of 3 different colors (red, blue, or green). Then the children were asked to follow a straightforward rule (eg, put the blue ones here and the other colors there). They then were asked to switch tasks (eg, put the cars here and the flowers there). Three-year-olds perseverated, or got stuck, on this task. They continued to the cards by the first rule. In this experiment, the 3-year-olds were then asked, "What is the rule?" and surprisingly, they could answer the question correctly most of the time. Yet, when told to once again follow that rule, they continued to follow the first plan, sorting by color. The same results were found when the prompts were reversed (shape and then color). Children this age understand but cannot implement the new rule; there seems to be too much complexity here for a 3-year-old.[11–13]

Four-year-olds are more capable of simultaneous processing. Most children this age easily switch from one paradigm (eg, colors, shapes) to the next. A 4-year-old can consider his options and respond appropriately, telling himself that "The color game is played this way and the shape game is played that way." Four-year-olds are able to reason, to consider multiple options, to learn from their mistakes, and to determine which option makes the most sense.

As children get older, they improve their ability to inhibit their responses. Another classic experiment features a child left in a room with a marshmallow. The researcher instructs the child that if he or she does not eat the marshmallow now, he or she will receive 2 marshmallows later. The studies demonstrate that at age 4 or 5 years, children start to show the capacity to inhibit the impulse to grab the marshmallow now and the reasoning skills to recognize that 2 treats later would be even better.

A mother asked me when her 7-year-old would stop sneaking her iPad. I told her that as long as she was giving him the password, he would keep using it, because for her 7-year-old, the immediate reward of the device had far more value than the fear of a later potential consequence.

Over the years, investigators have demonstrated the typical progression in human development of planning and organizational skills. This knowledge allows clinicians to provide parents with anticipatory guidance about a child's organizational trajectory. The dilemma, however, is that tremendous variation in **executive functioning** exists among children. Organizational development in one child does not predict for the progression in another. Fortunately, evidence shows that parenting and the environment in which a child is raised can influence a child's developmental progress.

Environmental Effects on Organization

Children are born with great potential, but how their brains develop depends in part on their exposures when they are very young. Inappropriate or under-stimulation of an infant or a toddler often leads to a child who has difficulty performing the routines of daily life. Particularly toxic environments, such as living with neglect, abuse, or exposure to violence, actually damage the brain, which results in angry outbursts when the child grows up.[14,15] The fear or stress caused by chaotic or unpredictable environments is hypothesized to trigger the release of cortisol, a hormone that at high enough levels can be toxic to the neuronal architecture (wiring) of the developing brain. Most of us can relate to this, because we have had the experience of being scared to the point that we do not think clearly or make good decisions. The damage caused by intense and chronic stress seems to be permanent.[15] So, prolonged exposure to difficult or frightening situations can harm the brain, while warm and supportive environments nourish the development of **executive function** skills. What exactly is meant by warmth and support, in the developing brain, is illustrated in future chapters of this book. While hugs and kisses are important, you will see that it is the comfort of consistency, the opportunity explore, and the challenge to try new things that is critical for raising an organized child.

As mentioned, trauma has permanent effects on the developing brain. Scientists have studied children raised in particularly difficult circumstances such as situations of abuse and neglect,[16] being raised in an orphanage,[17,18] and being born preterm or with perinatal complications.[19,20] Prenatal exposures, such as exposure to alcohol in utero, have a similarly damaging effect on the prefrontal cortex and other organizational structures of the brain. Subsequently, children who experience one or more of these toxic circumstances are much more likely to demonstrate impulsive and disorganized behavior as they get older. It is tragic to think that a child may experience more than one circumstance that may affect neurological development, but we see it all the time. For instance, a mother who has substance use disorder drinks and smokes during her pregnancy. Drugs and alcohol can sometimes lead to preterm deliveries. The new mother cannot afford or manage her newborn's needs and the child ends up in foster care or, if in another country, in an orphanage. Very likely, the child has been permanently affected.

Yet, do not despair for the child. We do know that a change in environment and the presence of at least one stable, nurturing adult in the first 1,000 days after birth can make a difference. Even children in foster care placements, who have less-frequent home transitions and are given more stable and consistent parenting, later tend to score better on measure of executive functioning.[21]

Environments that Support the Development of Organized Thinkers

The most supportive environments share qualities including responsive caregiving, consistency, and protection from sustained stress. Adults (both within the home and outside the home) foster the development of executive functions by showing confidence in the ability of a child and gradually encouraging the child to assume the "executive" role for herself. The trick is to support children with reasonable expectations that propel them forward at their own speed, but not too fast or too slow. Young children need greater supervision and scaffolding to organize the world around them, and as they get older, they need increasing opportunities to make decisions and mature.[4,5] It also seems that environments that are both more ordered and more predictable promote the development of executive functioning skills.[4,6] Later chapters of this book address specific interventions to support your child's organizational progress. The interventions challenge children to exercise their executive functioning skills.

Children whose executive functions have been supported do better at school and with peers. Studies show that children with stronger executive functions make greater progress on tests of early math, language, and literacy development during the preschool years. Executive functions contribute to academic learning, and advanced executive functions are also found in children with better social development.[22,23] The presumed explanation of this finding is that interpersonal skills place heavy demands on multitasking, self-control, planning, and other executive functions. The consequence of not being able to operate on the same cognitive or intellectual level as one's peers is often social isolation. Therefore, it is the parent's job to promote brain development, not with flash cards and tutoring, but through imagination, creativity, and play,[24–26] and specific activities are discussed in future chapters.

Researchers in the fields of developmental and behavioral pediatrics, neurology, psychology, and education continue to uncover new knowledge about the brain's executive functions. This book boils down some of that research into the most important 5 Steps to Raising an Organized Child, and these steps and interventions are described in the following chapters. Most of the evidenced-based interventions involve practical strategies, such as pretend play, that any parents can implement for their child. However, there are emerging, not yet proven computer-based technologies that may someday be shown to support the development of the executive functions. I recommend that you maintain a continuing dialogue with your pediatrician to keep abreast of new developments.

Improving Memory

Memory is the filing system of the brain and is therefore important for organized thinking. The memory system relies on a few simple principles to improve filing of new information and the retrieval of old memories:

duplication, meaningfulness, and rehearsal. Children with good memory systems perform these tasks subconsciously. However, these strategies can also be performed consciously, so that students can actively work to improve how they learn. Parents and teachers can demonstrate these techniques for students as they are learning to study.

Duplication

Memories are stored best when they are stored in numerous locations, making it easier to find the information later. When information is filed in several places, there are multiple context clues that can be used when it later needs to be retrieved. The simultaneous processing ability of the working memory allows for information to be sorted into multiple locations.

The working memory does this by instantaneously scanning the mental data banks to connect new lessons with related, previously learned information. For example, a teacher talking about tornadoes may trigger multiple connections in the child's brain. Even if the child has never before heard of a tornado, he may connect his new information to other types of deadly storms such as hurricanes and twisters. He may remember seeing the dust twirling on the playground and connect tornadoes to that event. He may recognize that *tornado* kind of sounds like *volcano* and a volcano is shaped like an upside-down tornado. He might even file his new knowledge next to his memories of munchkins and witches from *The Wizard of Oz.* Each of these locations is used for storage, but these storage sites then become triggers. Every time he thinks about the triggers, he potentially rehearses the memory of tornados. One key to memory is to actively think about new information, that is, to consider how it relates to what is already known. By actively doing this, the content is more likely to be stored in multiple locations.

Rehearsal

The more often a person accesses a memory, the better the connection comes. This phenomenon of rehearsal is best exemplified in sports. Some sport experts estimate that it takes 10,000 trials before a motor task, such as shooting a free throw in basketball, becomes automatic. Practice does pay off, and children that spend countless hours practicing always improve. The same is true for a toddler trying to walk, a preschool student learning the alphabet, a school-aged student starting to multiply, or a medical student memorizing the cranial nerves. Every teacher knows about rehearsal and practice, and most students have figured out that repetition is boring. So, teachers use numerous strategies to make rehearsal interesting and fun. When teaching the alphabet, teachers post the alphabet on the wall, students are asked to trace the letters, they sing the alphabet song, worksheets with phonological similarities are provided to students, and students are given simple picture books to look at, such as *A Is for Apple.* Parents can reinforce learning of the alphabet by using refrigerator magnets, rhyming, and pointing out letters on street signs. Exposing children to thousands of letters builds successful beginning readers.

Meaningfulness

One the most powerful strategies for making memories retrievable is to file them next to meaningful information. The goal is to connect new knowledge with prior information, and the more meaningful the previously stored information, the better. For instance, a student reading a book about Davy Crockett will be better able to remember what he has read if he can connect the new information with a vacation that his family took to Tennessee when his dad fell into a lake or his visit to the Alamo. In other words, information is learned best if it has meaning or value to the student.

Parents and teachers can make reading more memorable for students by helping young readers make connections. Before reading the book, parents can use context clues, such as the book cover or chapter titles, to encourage the child to make predictions about the book's content. When reading the book, parents should ask questions such as "What do you think will happen next?" or "Do you think Harry Potter would make a good friend?" The more ways the child thinks about what she is reading, and the more connected she feels to the story or its characters, improves consolidation and increases the likelihood of later retrieval.

Good teachers use advanced organizers to help students learn. An advanced organizer is an introductory statement that serves as a clue or a link between what was previously learned and what a student is about to be taught. For instance, a teacher might tell the class, "Remember when we discussed how the angles in a triangle always add up to 180 degrees? Well, today we are going to learn about the angles in a rectangle." A good basketball coach will also use advanced organizers when coaching a team. The coach might say, "Remember when we had a difficult time scoring last week against the other team's zone defense? Well, today I am going to show you a play that can be used to break that zone." Even before the coaching starts, the players should now have a picture in their minds as a frame of reference.

Chapter 2

The 5 Steps to Raising an Organized Child

Step 1: Be consistent

No matter what book you read or what parenting philosophy you adhere to, an overarching principal of good parenting is consistency. Parenting is about teaching, and any teacher can tell you that repeated exposures to a lesson works. Practice makes perfect...well, when it comes to children, almost perfect. Practice is important whether one is learning how to walk, write, shoot a basket, or behave. Repeated experiences of gentle redirection when needed and then positive feedback when a child takes steps in the right direction make up the fundamental principles of behavior training. Children gradually learn what is expected and how to behave with consistent parenting. Being consistent forms the foundation for all the other steps to raising an organized child. The 5 steps work only if they are performed consistently.

Alex was born in a Russian orphanage and adopted by his family when he was 10 months old. His parents reported that his first year with them was extremely difficult. They reported that he rarely slept for more than 3 hours at a time. The only way he could be soothed was to hold him or set him in a car seat on a washing machine until the vibration soothed him to sleep. When he was a toddler, he frequently threw tantrums, some of which would last for hours. As a preschool student, he was extremely impulsive and he was asked to leave 3 preschools before enrolling in kindergarten. In elementary school, he frequently visited the principal and there were times when the teachers made weekly calls to his parents to report his disruptive behavior.

It is very likely that the chaos Alex experienced during his time in the orphanage had long-lasting effects on his life. But here is the good news. Alex's parents were remarkably patient, loving, and consistent. They met all his physical needs with regular meals and comforting hugs. They did not overreact when Alex melted down, and they made his transitions to new schools as smooth as possible by visiting each school before his enrollment. Alex tended to push limits in elementary school, and his parents held firm on their boundaries, giving natural consequences for his behavior. In addition, this family gave Alex enrichment opportunities such as art and theater, and they read with him every night. By the time Alex became a sophomore in high school, things started to change. He became able to manage his homework and stopped getting into trouble. He graduated high school and went on to junior college where he earned high marks and transferred to a top university for his final 2 years before graduating. It took a long time, but consistent parenting paid off for Alex.

Predictability is soothing for most of us, while inconsistency and chaos are anxiety provoking. In fact, intense or chronic stress can be damaging to the developing brain. Consistent parents are predictable, and this puts children at ease, making them more receptive to learning and protecting them from stress, which causes the body to release stress hormones that can be toxic to the brain. A child of consistent parents can count on having her needs met and knows the boundaries of her behavior, because she can expect to be redirected or reprimanded when she breaks a rule. Conversely, she will also be consistently complimented for positive behavior. For an infant, having her needs met is comforting, and—even though it is hard to believe—telling a teenager "No" can be comforting too.

Even a consistently parented child can struggle with boundaries and limits. Be patient. Remember that organized thinking is a complex process; therefore, teaching a child organizational skills and to behave takes time. The goal is to raise a child into a happy and well-adjusted adult and not necessarily to have a "perfect child." Think about all the ways parents can be steady and reliable: nurturing a child, holding hands safely in a parking lot or when crossing the street, creating bedtime routines, limiting television time, enforcing a curfew, and emphasizing the importance of an education—just to name a few. There are so many routine opportunities to "act with consistency" that a parent needs to be vigilant. You don't want to be caught in a mistake and set an undesired precedent, which may be followed by months of cajoling (usually delivered with a "not fair" tone): "But you let me watch television during dinner before."

Along the way, it is easy for parents to develop their own ineffective behaviors, because sometimes, in the short run, they may work. Some parents might think screaming and spanking may get a quicker response from a child, but there are consequences to using this type of parental response. The American Academy of Pediatrics recommends that parents be encouraged to use methods other than spanking for managing undesired behavior. Research shows that spanking, slapping, and other forms of physical punishment don't work well to correct a child's behavior. First, these behaviors are scary for children and have the potential to cause harm to your child from extreme stress. Second, it is very difficult for a parent to use screaming and spanking consistently. These behaviors usually happen when a parent is being reactive and not planful, which makes consistency difficult. Third, yelling and screaming set a new limit, or threshold, for a child's behavior. The child's mind misinterprets the message. In other words, the child may think, "I don't have to turn off the television until Mom yells," or "I can keep screaming in the house until Dad says that he will spank me." Fourth, spanking models aggressive behavior to a child. If the most important person in a child's life hits (spanks) the child when that person is upset with her, she may think, "Hmm, hitting is OK." Instead, a consistent and firm approach is best in the long run when trying to teach lessons to children.

Although the principles of parenting remain throughout a child's life span, how a parent creates a stable environment varies across the developmental spectrum. Parents of infants must constantly meet a child's physical needs (eg, changing diapers, feeding) and emotional needs (eg, hugs when sad). As a child grows older, parents need to protect and should learn to react consistently during times of disappointment or frustration over their child's behavior. Inconsistent responses and overreactions are confusing to children who are trying to learn to deal with the consequences of their actions. As children become more aware and in control of their own behaviors, parents should use regular limit setting to clearly define expected behavior. Parents will need to continue this practice throughout the child's adolescence. Routines are important strategies that parents can implement to become even more consistent. In each chapter that follows, an overview and recommendations are provided for each age-group: infants, toddlers, preschoolers, school-aged children, and teenagers.

Step 2: Introduce order

At the simplest level, most of the tasks and actions we do can be reduced to a series of steps. Every undertaking, no matter how big or small, has a beginning, a middle, and an end. Or, in other words, a preparation phase, an action phase, and a restoration phase. For example, at mealtime, the food is prepared, next the food is served and eaten, and then the kitchen is cleaned. When playing, a game is set up, the game is played, and finally the game is put away. The concept of order is learned by repeated exposures from parents. Not surprisingly, this kind of order is not always readily apparent to some children. These children have trouble getting ready on time, stumble over getting started, and make seemingly careless mistakes because they consistently miss steps in procedures.

Nicole is a 12-year-old student whose parents were exasperated by her school performance. She had received "straight As" all through elementary school, but her grades dropped precipitously after entering middle school. She would earn high marks on tests, but her homework performance would bring down her grades. "The most frustrating part," Nicole's father told me, "is that she completes her homework but forgets to turn it in."

While Nicole struggled in middle school, there were earlier signs that sequential processing was difficult for her. First, Nicole had problems performing physical tasks that required a muscle memory plan. She played softball and had more difficulty learning to hit and throw a ball than did her peers, but catching was not a problem. Her printing was legible, but handwriting became so frustrating that she had given up on it by the fifth grade. Second, Nicole had difficulty following instructions. When she was a young girl, her parents and teachers recognized that they could give her only one task at a time. Asking her to brush her teeth, wash her face, and then put on her pajamas was an unrealistic request.

Nicole's story is common among students with poor sequential organization. Sequential processing relies on a part of the brain's memory system called the *sequential working memory.* Sequential working memory, also known as procedural memory, enables us to carry out commonly learned tasks without consciously thinking about them. It's our how-to knowledge. Riding a bike, tying a shoe, and washing dishes are all tasks that require procedural memory. Even what we think of as "natural" tasks, such as walking, require procedural memory; though we can do such tasks fairly easily, it's often hard to verbalize exactly how we do them. Procedural memory uses a different part of the brain than episodic memory (memory of experiences or specific events)—with brain injuries, a person can lose one ability without losing the other. That's why a person who has experienced amnesia and forgets much about his or her personal life often retains procedural memory: how to use a fork or drive a car, for example.

The working memory allows the brain to process more than one piece of information at a time and opens the door to organized thinking. For understanding order, this means that a child can be thinking about the next step while performing a task. The sequential working memory helps a child remember the order of tasks. This system of memory allows people to think forward and backward, enabling the development of foresight and hindsight. It allows children to understand the concept of time and gives them the ability to anticipate and even plan future actions. However, the development of the sequential memory system first requires a recognition of order and an understanding that all tasks have a beginning, a middle, and an end.

Recognizing Order

An observant parent is able to recognize symptoms of sequential disorganization when her child is still a very young child. A sequentially disorganized child does not recognize that there is a time component and an order to most daily routines. Preschool-aged children who take longer to learn common rituals, such as getting dressed in the morning or getting ready for bed in the evening, often have sequential processing deficits that get identified when they grow older, once late-elementary school and middle school put heavy demands onto the sequential working memory. For these students, the load of everyday tasks, such as getting ready on time, following instructions, coordinating movements, and completing schoolwork, may be overwhelming.

Teaching "step wisdom" to children actually begins during the newborn period and infancy, when parents consistently respond to the cries and needs of their baby. This responsiveness demonstrates cause (cry) and effect (response)—the first learned sequential thought. The baby learns when one thing occurs, something else naturally follows. Before babies even begin crawling, they figure out that ringing a bell makes a sound and making a cute noise generates a smiling response from a parent. For toddlers and preschoolers, excellent parents introduce concepts of time and teach the order inherent to every task. Parents of young children count often and show the procedural steps to tasks. They teach their preschoolers to finish activities by cleaning up. By the time a child enters school, she should understand that all tasks have a beginning, a middle, and an end. School-aged children learn to read, which reinforces a sequential approach to learning, by decoding one sound at a time and reading one word at a time. As they get older, they are guided to participate in planning, so that they can manage their homework. Teens are expected to perform long-range planning.

Understanding Time

Time is a sequence, and a student must learn to manage time: arrive to class on time and finish work on time. Students must also learn to break large assignments into smaller steps, making their task easier to accomplish, one step at a time. Young children are exposed to the words of time (eg, *later, tomorrow, yesterday, soon*). Older children are introduced to the units of time (eg, minutes, hours, days, years.) School-aged children are expected to track time, and older students learn to manage time. Students who master time are considered responsible.

The following chapters provide guidelines about age-appropriate expectations and strategies to challenge and promote the development of organizational skills at each level. It is important to remember that children will learn step wisdom and time management when order is introduced in their lives consistently and starting when they are very young.

Step 3: Give everything a place

Andy's mother calls him the "messiest 9-year-old on the planet." She says a bomb must go off in Andy's room each day shortly after he comes home

from school. Andy's mother has to follow him from school, to soccer prac-
tice, to home, picking up after him wherever he goes. She says that "Andy
cannot keep track of anything." Just 2 months into the school year, he has
already lost 2 jackets and a lunch box at school.

The third key to raising an organized child is to "Give everything a place," which helps children be prepared, but in a very different way than in the Step 2: Introduce order section earlier in this chapter. Sequential ordering has a temporal (time) component, whereas placement is all about knowing where things are when they are needed. The spatial working memory allows for the recognition, storage, and retrieval of large chunks of visual information. Spatial awareness means no more last-second, frantic searches for shoes before leaving the house or panicked hunts for your child's favorite toy anytime he wants it. Consider the possibility that an 8-year-old could clean up after playing a game or that a 12-year-old could make his bed and clean his room. Spatial organization means no more concerning calls from your child at school saying, "I forgot my lunch."

Location

Given the importance of spatial organization and planning, effective parents begin to teach spatial awareness during infancy, by giving things a place. At first, this is done by providing a stable setting for sleep and eating that is familiar to the child. For older children, toys are kept in specific locations. Parents should raise their spatial expectations as their children not only grow older but develop their abilities to know where things go. Preschool-aged children will need help cleaning up after themselves. Eventually, a spatially organized child should be able to maintain and keep her possessions tidy.

Spatial Language

Many spatial words are conceptual and more difficult to learn. Yet teaching the spatial language is another way to reinforce spatial awareness. Spatial words designate the size and shape of objects. Prepositions (eg, *behind, below, beneath, between*) are used to describe positioning relative to other objects, and they give a preschooler another way to think about and organize her world. School-aged children learn to follow and give directions. This knowledge will help them understand graphs and maps when they get older.

Spatial Chunking (Grouping)

Spatial processing is a very efficient system for "chunking together" information in the brain, because multiple pieces of information can be recorded as an isolated mental image. Things that would take paragraphs to describe can be summed up by one picture. Certain types of information are best recorded spatially, as a mental picture, into the memory instead of sequentially. For instance, when a child walks into a classroom on the first day of school, he is immediately exposed to many new images. He sees the desks placed neatly in the middle of the room, each with a name tag and a little blue chair, all pointed toward a large desk at the front of the classroom. He notices that each wall is decorated with a different theme. One wall has letters; another, pictures of countries; and so on. It would be unproductive and unrealistic to sequentially identify each desk and every wall decoration, one at a time. Instead, the brain keeps a mental picture and therefore chunks the visual information together automatically, a very efficient system for remembering things.

Academic Spatial Awareness

Spatial processing becomes increasingly sophisticated and important for a school-aged child. Children who develop a visual approach (sight-word reading) read faster. Even the foundation of reading, phonetic decoding, or recognizing that a sound corresponds to specific groups of letters requires visual processing and memory. Visualization of what is read helps students comprehend and remember. Math students have an advantage when they can visualize math concepts and understand graphs. And of course, athletes with strong visual processing systems are often better at playing ball sports. Because the ways one uses the visual system to process academics, music, and athletics are all related, research supports the idea that involvement in any of these can improve performance in the others. The uses for spatial memory and processing span many domains such as reading, math, and athletics and play a critical role in the development of an organized child.

Step 4: Practice forward thinking

What is meant by the term *forward thinking?* Forward thinking is organized thought about the future. It is much more difficult to think about tomorrow than it is to think about today. For example, it may be easy to decide what you feel in the moment like eating, but it is a much more difficult task to predict what you will feel like having for lunch tomorrow. Likewise, it is easy to put on a jacket if it feels cold outside, but it requires more-sophisticated thought to plan a wardrobe for a weekend adventure. Children have problems executing forward thinking until about age 4 years, and even teenagers are notably weaker at it than adults. Yet glimmers of forward-thinking skills are apparent in very young children.

> *My daughter and I participated in a camping group for 5- to 10-year-old girls and their dads. My entire family had camped together, but this was the first time my daughter and I would share our own tent. When we arrived at the campsite, I quickly unloaded our things and then greeted the other dads assuming that my daughter would link up with her friends. But when I checked in on her 15 minutes later, she had set up the tent and outfitted it with our sleeping bags and pillows. In her 5-year-old mind, she had created and executed a plan of what should happen first when camping.*

In the following chapters, I describe important forward-thinking organizational skills such as anticipating, predicting, planning, and estimating. Children begin to use these skills once they develop foresight and hindsight—the ability to think forward and backward. With these new abilities, they can use their prior experience and knowledge to consider the best option for the future. Children with neurodevelopmental conditions such as attention-deficit/hyperactivity disorder, cognitive impairment, Down syndrome, fetal alcohol syndrome, and autism often have problems with forward thinking and more difficulty learning from their mistakes, and that's OK. Children with these conditions will make progress, but their rate of progress may be slower. Remember that mistakes are learning experiences and as parents we are teachers. Punishing them for their mistakes is not the solution. Parents will need to be patient. Explain the mistake, discuss future options, and give them the opportunity to succeed. Consistency is critical, because children learn from repetition. Children develop the ability to think ahead in gradual stages. Before entering preschool at around age 4, children are capable of very little planning. Planning becomes more common practice for children at around age 6, and by age 10, they are capable of fairly sophisticated planning, but many 10-year-olds use this skill inconsistently. Lack of practice leads to atrophy (weakening of the brains planning "muscles"), and so a wide variation in planning skills exists among teenagers.

Hindsight and Foresight

As I mentioned, forward thinking is complicated because it requires simultaneous processing. Hindsight and foresight are the foundation for thinking ahead and require multilevel cognitive processing (requires the integration of many brain regions responsible for thought). To think ahead, a child needs to recognize the difference between the present or past and the future. Once a child begins to consider the past (hindsight) and the future (foresight), he becomes more capable of making a logical guess or an estimate.

Predicting and Estimating

Estimation is the forward-thinking process of finding a value that is usable for some purpose even if the data are incomplete. Children are formally taught to estimate in math, but people also use estimation for many other purposes. Estimates are important when making predictions about how to act, behave, or perform in the future. For example, a child may think that it was cold yesterday, so she decides to bring a jacket today. Likewise, a student who is not entirely sure how a new teacher may want the title page of a report formatted can make a prediction using what other teachers have wanted in the past. Considering the past while making a prediction is a valuable quality of an organized thinker.

Anticipating

Anticipating is a skill that is critical for behavior and social successes and can happen only when a child thinks forward. A child who can remember routines or schedules can then expect an outcome. As fun as a surprise can be, most children like them only when they result in something great such as a sudden trip to Disneyland. Kids like predictability, and a child who is unskilled at thinking ahead, and not able to anticipate, lives in an unpredictable world. Unpredictable change is difficult for many to tolerate, and for some, it is like torture, throwing the child into "meltdown mode." These children need constant routine transitions throughout their day, such as when departing for school, when washing hands before eating, and when getting ready for bed. As I have pointed out, children have problems forward thinking before age 5 years, and that is why children between the ages of 2½ and 4½ have particular difficulty tolerating change. There is wide variation among the ages at which children learn to be flexible—some adults still struggle with flexibility! Parents can help children learn to anticipate by using schedules and encouraging them to practice forward thinking.

Planning

As a general rule, parenting forward thinking can be divided into stages. Before age 5 years, consistency is used to familiarize children with routines, and during this time, parents can model planning for children. A parent might say, for instance, "Let's clean up the toys first, then get dressed, and after that we can go to the park." By sharing a plan out loud, she is modeling a very important skill for the young child. After a child turns 5, parents can challenge a child to think ahead. In this instance, a parent might offer, "Let's go to the park, but what should we do before we go?" This suggestion may be enough to cue the child to formulate his own plan, especially if a consistent pattern has been established. "Clean up and get dressed," says your child, who might even suggest bringing his favorite toy or the family dog for a walk. By the time a child turns 10, parents should challenge their child to make plans for many life routines: not only being prepared for school and sports but planning homework and playtime. Teenagers can be challenged to plan for the future. They can visualize goals and can consider the steps needed to obtain those objectives.

Planning is automatic to many adults, but it is a very difficult skill to master. Our job as parents is to encourage our children to practice their planning skills. Children need to have the opportunity to make plans. These days, the daily schedule of children is so busy that they do not have the opportunity to think for themselves. When they have some free time, many default to electronic games that are automated and do most of the thinking for the child. School-aged children need to practice arranging playdates so that they can learn to make plans with a friend. Middle school students should be planning what to do with their extra weekend time, and teenagers ought to be able to manage their own schedules. When parents do not hand over control or they allow students to default to electronics, children miss out on planning practice.

Some children will resist using these skills, because like anything new, forward thinking can be difficult. While growing up, children will make hundreds of miscalculations along the way. There will be times when it may be easier for parents to do things for their child, but be careful and resist this urge whenever possible. Let your child learn from his or her mistakes, especially when your child is young and the consequences are minimal. By letting your children struggle with some choices when they are younger, you empower independence over time, and you will be more confident about their ability to make choices as a teenager, when the stakes are higher. Forward thinking does not just happen; it is a learned skill, and parents can be vigilant about teaching this process to their children.

Step 5: Promote problem-solving

Think about the most organized person you know. Envision a friend who gracefully handles many different tasks all at once. Maybe he is the dad who coaches his daughter's soccer team. Or maybe she is the classroom volunteer for her son and holds a part-time job. The children of these parents are rarely late for an appointment, and these parents often volunteer to bake brownies for fun events. Integral to being organized is being able to handle multiple things at one time. For me, I think about a colleague of mine who always seemed to have a good answer. When I was preparing a presentation, he knew what points to emphasize. When I was planning out research, he helped focus my research question. When it came time to study for an examination, he knew what would be on the test. My colleague has a brilliant grasp of the big picture, just like a supermom or a superdad has a wonderful awareness of everything going on around her or him. Organized thinkers are gifted with working memories that allow them to store information and smoothly shift back and forth between multiple thoughts without a neurological glitch. This allows them to consider many possibilities, see the big picture, and create the best plan.

We cannot all be a superparent or brilliant scientist, but we can use our organizational skills to solve the problems of the daily tasks that come at us all at once. From a child's perspective, problem-solving challenges are everywhere. Answering questions such as "How can I write this essay?" "What would my boyfriend like for a Christmas gift?" and "What should I do when I am bored?" requires the brain to simultaneously perform multiple cognitive functions. Conquering boredom, considering options, creating a story, or taking perspective, amongst many other complicated skills, demands simultaneous use of sophisticated language processing, organized memory retrieval, and planning. The working memory, the brain's mental whiteboard, is heavily challenged while problem-solving. Fortunately, as mentioned previously, the working memory can be strengthened with practice and brain exercise, and that effort can make your child a better problem-solver.

That is why parenting directive number 5 is to "Promote problem-solving" with your child. In other words, encourage your child to think about and figure out the big picture for himself. Do not do everything for him. Parents can actually stunt their child's cognitive development by doing too much for their child. Do not overschedule your child; instead, occasionally allow your child to have "nothing to do." This can be very positive, because he will need to figure out, on his own, what to do with his time. When developmentally appropriate, allow your child to make his own decisions, big or small. Challenge him to organize his thoughts, grasp the big picture, think flexibly, be imaginative, and be social. These skills have often been referred to as *higher-order cognitive functions,* because of the complicated interplay of neurocognitive functions (multiple brain regions responsible for thought) they demand.

Imagination and Creativity

Imagination is an organizational challenge, because thinking creatively requires the formation of a mental plan. Creativity is more complicated than linear thinking tasks, such as mapping a driving route from one location to another. Imagination deals with multiple variables: abstract ideas, memory of prior events, the future, and sometimes unlimited possibilities. Simple creative thoughts begin when children are young. For instance, many children, between the ages of 2 years and 3 years, learn to role-play. As children begin to pretend, they may, at first, default to the same script. For example, they may always want Thomas the Tank Engine to get stuck going up the mountain. They struggle when a parent or another child tries to introduce a variable scenario. As children get older, their role-playing becomes both more complex and more creative. For instance, when my daughters were all playing together at ages 8, 6, and 3 years, they would create schools, build unique Lego worlds, and script their own plays. Even the 3-year-old could understand that her role varied with each situation.

Flexible Thinking

Flexible thinking is another higher-order cognitive function. To arrive at the best conclusion, a person needs to be able to consider multiple possibilities. There are often many ways to solve a problem (eg, how to answer an essay question, what to play on a rainy day, who gets the last piece of dessert), and there are many increasing complex social considerations that can be made when coming to a conclusion. Flexible thinking includes thinking about efficiencies, practicalities, and the feelings of others.

As children grow older, they become capable of more-flexible thought. Two-year-old children, for example, are classically inflexible thinkers. A 2-year-old who is trying to build something with blocks might repeat the same mistake, giving up or getting frustrated. At age 4 or 5 years, children are more capable of problem-solving for other design options. Yet, they are still not very good at compromise because their perspective-taking skills remain limited. Young children tend to be rule governed, and it is very difficult for them to have flexible thinking. Many young children see things as right or wrong and struggle with anything in between.

Inflexible thinking has been associated with negative behavior. Inflexible thinkers struggle to cope with unmet expectations and therefore have problems with changes in plans, transitions, and sometimes losing games. To avoid the frustration caused by things not going their way, they play by themselves or, when in groups, they insist on doing things their own way. The solution is to teach children to think flexibly by teaching problem-solving skills.

Years ago, I worked with a teenager and his mother who were at odds over the effort the teen gave to his homework and the mother's need to supervise. As the situation escalated, this teen, like many teens before him, insisted on more independence and said that "Mom is controlling my life." The mother's argument was that the teen "didn't care about anything." I encouraged the problem-solving process by getting them to describe what each of them specifically wanted. The mother wanted to be sure the son was doing his homework. The son didn't want to be "nagged" about homework. So, I laid the dilemma out for the son, "What could you do to get your mother to stop nagging you?" After a brief discussion, the solution was that if the mother would leave him alone, the son would do his homework independently, and when finished he would leave it on the kitchen table before 7:30 pm. If the homework was not there by 7:30 each night, the mom was free to "pester" the son. Problem almost solved, until I pointed out that in this compromise the son was doing all the work and Mom just had to remain quiet. So, I asked what would happen if the mother pestered before 7:30 pm. The son decided that because he liked baby carrots, the mother could buy a bag of these treats for him each time she prematurely nagged. Both were able to be flexible once I was able to get them to articulate their stressors.

Three weeks later, the same teen returned to my office looking dejected and the mother cautioned him about his messy bathroom. So I said, "You want his bathroom to be clean and he wants you to stop pestering him," and before I could finish, the teenager said, "I know. If I can clean my bathroom every other day before 7:30 pm, she will get me more carrots if she pesters me." The teen was seeing things more clearly than the mother. Perhaps it was all the carrots he had been eating! Teaching children to be flexible when solving problems makes it much easier for everyone to behave.

Perspective Taking

Learning to be social can be a difficult problem to solve for some children. Sharing and dealing with the feelings of others is counterintuitive. To a child who has not yet matured, it makes the most sense to always get to go first, not share toys, and always "be right." The concept of "the greater good" has no meaning to a young or inflexible person. One of the first social skills taught is to take turns. How do you explain turn taking to a child who thinks that his way is the only one way to do things? Preschool children can consider that there may be multiple ways to do something, but they are just starting to learn how to take perspective or consider the opinions of others and therefore often come to the conclusion that their way is best. Taking perspective, or to coin a phrase from Speech and Language Pathologist Michelle Garcia Winner's work, "Thinking about You Thinking about Me," is complicated. Good social thinkers consider not only their own experience but also the prior knowledge of their audience. Demonstrating perspective sometimes means choosing an option that is less beneficial to oneself. For instance, a socially adept childhood friend may realize that his buddy has gotten picked last for a competition 3 times in a row and so decide to choose him first, even at the expense of losing a game, because the greater good might be making his friend feel better. Many arguments and prejudices stem from poor perspective taking. The more we share other perspectives and ideologies with our children, the better they will become at understanding the thoughts of others. As with any problem-solving skill, practice is required to improve. Parents should model perspective taking for their child.

Conquering Boredom

Creativity and flexible thinking are required to conquer boredom. A child with limited creativity skills may default to 1 or 2 preferred activities (eg, television and video games) when he is bored, and if you take away those preferred options, he is miserable. Children who are engaged and interested are better at accessing a variety of cognitive options to conquer boredom. In a sense, they have an organized "drop-down menu" of things in their brains that they can do when they are bored at home or in class. The drop-down menus of the brain are comparable to how computers are organized. When an organized child is confronted with a dilemma such as free time, he accesses a metaphorical mental drop-down menu of options. But when this menu does not spontaneously appear for a child who lacks organization, he chooses to respond with the first action that pops into his mind. In the case of a 2-year-old, for instance (because 2-year-olds are by definition disorganized thinkers), the response is usually no. When this behavior continues beyond the age of 5 years, it is problematic. Sometimes the problem is not oppositional behavior; it stems from a lack of a functional, instantaneous mental drop-down menu system. Children often appear bored, because they cannot consider a mental list of activities to do.

Brain development is fascinating in that sometimes one part of the brain develops at the expense of another. It is not uncommon to find disorganized but gifted (also known as "twice exceptional") students. Parents of these children often tell me that their child is so smart that she is bored at school; their assumption is that the teacher is not stimulating their child enough. While it may be true that a teacher who is responsible for 30 students with a range of abilities is not constantly keeping the top 2% of the class engaged, in most cases, I do not believe that unengaging teaching is the root cause of most students' boredom. In fact, I treat many talented students who are never bored. Disinterested students often have disorganization as a common issue: they get bored because they cannot access a drop-down menu of ideas that they want to think about to fill the academic void. On the other hand, to combat boredom, an organized child might, for example, make plans for after-school fun, compose a mental love song, remember everyone who played for the 2004 World Series Champion Boston Red Sox, or think about all the things he could do with worms. In some ways, efforts to battle boredom are similar to how components of the imagination or creativity systems work. Effective creativity can be described as the organized mental search for related, but unique, ideas. Thus, the importance of the junction between memory and the executive functions (the brain's ability to plan, organize, and complete tasks) is great, as it influences not only a child's behavior but also his creativity and academic output.

Do not be afraid to let your child be bored. Solving boredom is exercise for the brain. So, resist the urge to pull out the iPhone when he starts to squirm. Instead, show him how to create fun.

Big Picture Thinking

I consider the ability to grasp the big picture the ultimate step in organized thinking. Big picture thinkers often make great leaders because they can balance a team's goal with the individual goals of the participants. Many adults never acquire the capacity to step back and take a broader view of a situation, so a child who can do this is very advanced. Being generous is an early sign that a child understands the big picture, because taking the perspective of another person requires thinking about what someone else might like. Summarization is a straightforward example of complex organized thinking. Telling another person about what has happened seems simple enough, but a good summary is more than just an account of what has occurred. In addition to recalling the events, the speaker should have an understanding of the audience's understanding of the subject.

For example, in teaching my daughter about Thanksgiving, I could say that Thanksgiving is a holiday that started after pilgrims facing religious persecution in Europe came to America for a free place to live. Once they arrived in America, they met Native Americans and together they had a feast of thanks. However, if my daughter has no prior knowledge of pilgrims, Europe, or religious persecution, she will be confused. Because I know that about my daughter in advance, I could instead define those points in my summary. For instance, a more appropriate summary might be as follows: Thanksgiving is a holiday that started after people living in another part of the world, called Europe, sailed across the ocean to America. They left Europe because the rulers did not allow them to pray the way they wanted. When they arrived in America, they met Native Americans, people who already lived in America, and together they had a great feast to give thanks for their good fortune. Model summarizing and encourage your child to summarize his experiences to demonstrate his understanding of the big picture.

Problem-solving is a sophisticated skill that develops gradually over a lifetime, but you put the building blocks into place for this skill when children are young. Start encouraging your child to think now, tomorrow, and every day after that. The following chapters describe developmentally appropriate suggestions to practice problem-solving with your child.

Chapter 3

Raising an Organized Infant: The Bonding Years

Step 1: Be consistent

An infant's total dependence on parents makes meeting her needs the focus of early parenting. Parents must be responsive to her physical and emotional needs in a consistent and predictable manner. Fortunately, it doesn't take much to nurture an infant: swaddling, smiles, and a soothing voice. Consistency is fundamental to learning. By being responsive to an infant's physical and emotional needs, parents set their infant up for success. A lack of nurturing can have devastating effects on an infant. I have worked with many children who have had the misfortune to live in a foreign orphanage where often, up to 6 infants share a single crib, a caregiver comes by once an hour to check diapers, and 3 times a day the infants are given a bottle.

Consistent parenting and nurturing reduces an infant's exposure to toxic stress. Parents who can understand the different cries of their baby (eg, hunger, fussy, wet diaper), and who respond to those cries appropriately, teach their baby that when she cries, she is comforted. So, parents should change diapers, support sleep, and feed their baby as needed.

The cry causes the response. This reinforces to the child that her specific cry is a form of communication.

When parents are consistent, there is a bond formed with the child that makes her feel secure. By 10 months of age, infants have clearly preferred caregivers and show signs of stranger anxiety when handed off to an unfamiliar face. Some stranger anxiety is a very appropriate reaction for a child this age, and in fact, a complete lack of stranger anxiety can be a reason for concern and worth a consultation with your pediatrician. Consistent parenting establishes a wonderful infant-parent bond and sets the child up for a lifetime of positive experience.

During the newborn period and infancy, babies begin to learn that there is order to the world around them. Over the first 8 months after their birth, they learn the concept of cause and effect. In other words, they understand their first sequences as infants. They also learn about their environment and become increasingly comfortable with the world around them. They recognize that being placed into their bed means it is time to sleep, their high chair signals that it is time to eat, and their changing table means wait for Daddy to remove the diaper and then pee all over him. And this all depends on parents being consistent.

The toys to choose for babies at this age can reinforce the cause and effect relationship. By 8 months of age, most infants have an understanding of cause and effect and quickly learn to play with toys that reinforce that principle. These toys do not need to be technologically advanced; the simple toys are often best, such as pop-up toys and the jack-in-the-box. Pushing buttons and twisting levers to make noise can give infants positive feedback they desire and can tell them that every action has a reaction.

☑ Consistency Recommendations for Infants

- Respond promptly to your baby's cries of discomfort.
  - Address your baby's needs for comfort: food, sleep, and diaper changes.
- Establish routines for your infant's sleep and hunger.
  - Feeding routines can be established at set times and in set locations. Limit distractions during feeding. Parents can comfort their child by feeding in a calm and quiet environment.
  - Infants should be encouraged to sleep at a routine time and in a routine location.
  - Parents should implement regular, calming routines before bedtime.
- The most appropriate toys for infants are the classic "cause and effect" toys, which allow the child to explore and identify an object and its function. They signal a baby's ability to exert influence and should begin to be introduced at around 3 months of age.
  - The simplest toys are rattles and swinging toys that the infant can bat with a hand and that can squish and make sounds.
  - When a young child is 6 months, the cause and effect toys can be more sophisticated to encourage the child to twist or push the object in a particular direction in order to get a response (eg, a noise, music, or a pop-up toy).

Step 2: Introduce order

Babies learn at an exponential rate during their first few months after birth, and the first organizational concept that a child learns is cause and effect, a foundation for learning sequences. At just a few days old, newborns can recognize their mother's voice. Soon, they learn how to soothe themselves by sucking their fingers or thumb. Infants demonstrate their understanding of sequences before age 1 year; thus, training of sequencing should begin when a child is an infant. During this phase, parents introduce the concept of cause and effect and model order by establishing routines, and by the time the child becomes a toddler, they introduce the language of order.

Consistent Parenting

Parents who can consistently meet the needs of their child are unknowingly teaching order to their child. A social smile is a cause and effect interaction. If a family member smiles at the child, she should smile back. In fact, the lack of a social smile in a 6-month-old is a red flag for a potential developmental concern that should prompt a parent to seek support from a pediatrician. Parents of newborns should spend time watching their newborn's face. When your baby makes a face, get close and make the face back. When your baby sticks out her tongue, you do it too, and when she starts to babble and coo, imitate that sound back to your child. Your baby will find your faces funny by a few months of age and sometimes laugh out loud. Between 3 months old and 6 months old, she will imitate you as you imitate her. In a sense, you will have had your first nonverbal conversation with your baby just by enjoying each other's faces. No matter the lesson, feeding, diaper changing, play, or communication, babies will continue to learn best with consistency.

Teaching Cause and Effect

At 6 to 7 months old, infants learn to perform their first 2-step sequences. For instance, they can perform an action such as shaking a bell, and this action causes the bell to ring. The child does something and gets a response. As they continue to explore their world, they bang and mouth everything they can touch. The noise that follows the banging is an example of cause and effect. They appreciate the sound and so they bang more. Most infants learn this concept independently, but the way parents respond, and the toys they offer, to their child can solidify this concept in their child's mind.

Increasing Sequence

Start playing 2-step games with your baby now too. Many 6-month-olds enjoy peekaboo and "peep eye." With peekaboo, you cover your face with your hands and say, "Where is Daddy?" Then, opening your hands, you declare, "Here I am!" The peep eye game is when you cover your child with a blanket and say, "Where is Cassie?" and then pull the blanket off and say, "There she is!" Before the age of 1 year, your daughter will learn to pull the blanket off by herself, because she understands the order of the game. You will see her understanding as she begins to smile in preparation for the game. Another sequential game that infants at the age of 9 months will enjoy is pat-a-cake. The sequential order of "Pat it," "Roll it," and "Mark it with a B" will be of great enjoyment to your child.

The toys we buy for our young children should serve more of a purpose than being just for fun. Infants and toddlers need "cause and effect" toys to build their sequencing skills. Try not to get caught up in the hype about battery-operated gadgets, with all the lights and noise. The classic toys offer all the sophistication an infant needs. Little babies are given mobiles so that they can bat at and cause the toys to move. They are given rattles to shake, which make noise, and toys with buttons that, when pushed, respond in some manner. A jack-in-the-box or other pop-up toys are classic cause and effect builders, and they come without batteries.

Establishing Routines

The routines that affect physiology, such as sleeping, eating, and, when a child gets older, toilet training, are other perfect places to start learning order. Parents cannot introduce regular routines too soon. In fact, some sleep experts recommend introducing sleep routines shortly after a baby comes home from the hospital. Beyond the importance of training cause and effect, the comfort given to your baby by the consistency of a bedtime routine offers the child a sense that everything will be OK. So later on, down the road, when parents decide to let their child cry himself to sleep, for instance, their child may protest, but he will also have a sense of security that if he really needed something, his parents will provide it to him.

In addition, parents that offer routine feeding times can train their infant's body biorhythms (internal cycles that regulate memory, temperament, emotions, and much more, which in turn keeps physiological stress at bay). Unknowingly, regular feedings are setting an infant's biological clock. Since learning the concept of time is a critical organizational milestone, developing the internal clock is important.

Consistent comforting from parents, the implementation of routines, playing simple games, and using toys all contribute to the development of a baby's understanding of sequencing.

 Sequencing Recommendations for Infants

Consistent Parenting

■ Parents should learn to respond to their child in a calm and consistent manner. Babies cry to communicate their needs, which tend to be as simple as sleep, eat, and "pee/poop." When a newborn or an infant is not content, parents can use the following steps when considering their child's needs:

  ■ Check to see whether your baby's diaper needs to be changed.

  ■ Feed your baby if it is an appropriate feeding time or if you believe she is genuinely hungry.

  ■ Hold and gently try to burp your baby.

  ■ Rock, sway, and sing to her softly.

  ■ Try moving to a new location (eg, go to another room, walk outside) or adjust her position.

  ■ Allow her to sleep.

  ■ If this doesn't work, start the list over, but be patient. Sometimes babies act fussy, cry, and are hard to console.

Establishing Routines

■ Implement regular routines for daily activities such as feeding, nap time, bathing, and bedtime. For instance, a typical nap time procedure for a 4-month-old infant should include a familiar setting (such as the infant's room), turning down the lights, holding the infant in a familiar position, singing the same song or reciting the same story, and then laying the infant into her bed.

Teaching Cause and Effect

■ Introduce "cause and effect" toys.

  ■ For infants, aged 1 to 6 months, consider toys that move when pushed or make noise when manipulated.

  ■ By the time your baby is 8 months of age, start to introduce toys that require an element of planning, such as the classic jack-in-the-box or the "pop-up pals."

  ■ Introduce cause and effect games such as "peep eye" and peekaboo by the time your baby is 6 months old.

Understanding Time

■ Use finishing words and songs that emphasize termination and closure, such as "cleanup" and "bye-bye."

Step 3: Give everything a place

The brain of a child undergoes tremendous growth during the first few years after birth. The visual cortex is the part of the brain important for recognizing and understanding what we see. The visual cortex of an infant is not fully developed. Research has proven that parents can significantly affect the growth of this part of the brain by presenting the infant with visually contrasted objects.[27] The best way you as a parent can stimulate your baby's vision is by using black-and-white stripes or light-and-dark contrasting colors (eg, red, white, and black.) Whoever started decorating nurseries with pretty soft pastels was not an ophthalmologist. Grandparents may love those colors, but they unfortunately do nothing for a baby. Surround a baby with soft pastel colors, and you might as well be blindfolding him. High contrast is much more valuable to the development of an infant's brain.

A stimulated infant will learn and grow at a remarkable pace. Just days after babies are born, they learn to turn their head toward a voice, thereby demonstrating their recognition that a stimulus can correspond with a location. Spatial awareness is clearly forming in an older infant who is beginning to explore his surroundings. He reaches for nearby objects and observes people as they enter the room. Encourage the development of your child's spatial awareness by talking to him from different parts of the room, and watch him localize the sound. Then smile at him, and after a few months of age, he will recognize the pattern of your smile and smile back.

Another significant visual milestone is the development of object permanence. Object permanence is the ability of a child to remember that something out of his sight actually still exists. A 7-month-old infant typically understands object permanence. An example is when an infant drops a spoon from her high chair; she then looks over the edge to see where it has gone. Before that age, things that are out of sight are literally out of mind. With the onset of object permanence, it is clear that a baby now has the ability to hold in her mind the location of an object. Between the ages of 8 months and 12 months, if you ask infants whether they want to eat food, they may turn their head toward the refrigerator, because they know that is where food is kept. If you tell infants that it is time for bed, they may instinctively lean toward their crib. If they can learn to recognize the location of these objects, without any intentional teaching from a parent, think about what your infant is capable of learning with consistent parental efforts to teach the location of objects. Giving objects a place allows your children to learn that items will be where they expect them to be when they want them.

☑ Spatial Recommendations for Infants

- Infants need visual contrast. Decorate your baby's room with light-and-dark stripes.
  - Highly contrasting baby mobiles grab your baby's attention while she is awake. Similarly, choose toys for infants such as rattles and first teddy bears that use contrast instead of soft colors.
- Babies spend most of their time asleep, but when your child is awake, give him something to look at. A parent's face is a perfect object for his attention. Move your face back and forth and watch how your infant will follow you with his gaze.
  - Hold your child in a way that encourages face-to-face contact. Because watching facial expressions promotes the development of spatial awareness, let your child watch changes in parental facial expressions.
- During early infancy, try to establish consistent locations for feeding, sleeping, and diaper changing.
- Parents should begin to organize the infant's spatial world. Identify spots for toys, clothes, bath toys, stuffed animals, and more.
- Play peekaboo or "peep eye" when young children develop object permanence at around 7 to 8 months old.

Step 4: Practice forward thinking

The brain of an infant is not yet mature enough to perform forward thinking. Babies live in the moment. They eat when they are hungry. They sleep when they are tired. They do almost no planning or anticipating. However, the foundation needed for planning and anticipating is created during this period by promoting the understanding of cause and effect. Once a child comprehends that one thing leads to the next, he can at first expect an outcome and second, when older, predict or anticipate a result. By following the suggestions listed under the "Sequencing Recommendations for Infants" box earlier in this chapter, such as being predictable and playing games such as peekaboo, infants learn to anticipate what comes next.

Step 5: Promote problem-solving

A newborn has all the brain cells needed to perform complicated thought, but most of the neural networks are not connected. Your consistent efforts to meet the needs of your baby actually help the brain make connections. Infants are not yet capable of problem-solving; however, they are able to learn some of the foundational skills for problem-solving such as social responsiveness and cause and effect. Parents can model social responsiveness as they care for their child, exhibiting that an awareness of their child's behavior can dictate a parental response. Parents can also model another problem-solving skill, flexible thinking, by making adjustments when addressing the needs of their baby (eg, if changing a diaper does not calm a baby, consider feeding, singing to, or rocking the baby). Parents should watch the eyes and face of their child. Infants have a tremendous ability to imitate facial expressions. Make faces at your child. This imitative play helps lay the groundwork for pretending during the toddler years.

☑ Recommendations to Teach Problem-solving to Infants

- Respond promptly to a baby's cries of discomfort. Address your baby's needs for comfort: proper clothing for the temperature, hunger, sleep, and diaper changes.
- "Cause and effect" toys should begin to be introduced at around 3 months of age.
  - The simplest toys are rattles and swinging toys that an infant can bat with a hand.

- When a young child is 6 months old, the cause and effect toys can be more sophisticated to encourage the child to twist or push the object in a particular direction in order to get a response (eg, a noise, music, or a pop-up toy).

- By responding calmly and making parenting adjustments as needed, parents can be a model of flexible thinking for their child.

- Make eye contact with your child.

  - Make faces at your child and imitate the faces that your child makes. By imitating the faces that your child makes, you teach him that his actions have an influence on others and reinforce the importance of eye contact.

- When your infant can roll, scoot, or crawl, place toys just out of reach and let her figure out how to reach them.

Chapter 4

Raising an Organized Toddler: The Great Explorers

The toddler years are a period of tremendous developmental growth. Toddlers can range in age from 1 year to 3 years. During these years, your child will begin to walk and talk, and, before you know it, she will be running and conversing. The onset of greater movement and language exponentially increases your child's ability to learn about the world around her, and the best way for a toddler to learn is through play. Your toddler's play skills will increase dramatically, and by the time your toddler turns 3, she will be capable of performing pretend and imaginative play.

Most toddlers are inherently social. Often, it seems that their No. 1 priority is to connect with their family around them. They watch what we do and then they learn to imitate us. If Dad is in the kitchen cooking, they love to pretend to be making a meal too, and when Mom is cleaning, toddlers will want to push their toy vacuum around too. But when a parent is sleeping, well, unfortunately, that is where imitation ends and play begins, because they want to wake us up. I recall on one occasion kissing my wife in front of my toddler and, instantly, there was a set of puckered 2-year-old lips pushing their way between us. Our toddlers watch our every move and love being social, but when they do not seem interested in those around them, that can be a sign of a more significant medical issue that should be discussed with your pediatrician.

Step 1: Be consistent

Your toddler is watching and observing you and learning everything about you, such as the tone of your voice, the calmness of your responses, the rules you follow, the way you act toward others, and the choices you make. Hopefully, as a parent, you are modeling skills that you want your child to acquire. The more often and the more consistently a behavior occurs, the easier it will be for your child to learn it. On the other hand, inconsistent and erratic parental responses and choices disrupt the educational process. I find that in families who are stressed out and overworked, their priority becomes making it through each day. These parents can tend to take parenting shortcuts such as taking their toddler for a drive in the car to help him fall asleep, instead of teaching their child to consistently nap in his own bed. Or parents sometimes feel it's easier to clean up after their toddler because it is quicker, instead of teaching their child to clean up after himself. I understand that life can be complicated, but the guiding principal for parenting is to "Be consistent."

Now that toddlers are walking, their ability to move quickly can put them into unsafe situations, and it is up to parents to keep them safe. At this stage, parents should begin to set consistent limits. Some limits are toddler specific, using safety gates to help them avoid any stairs they might fall down. Parents will want to use outlet covers so that toddlers can't stick anything into the electrical socket. It is very important at this age that toddlers start to learn that the word *no* is important, and "No" really does mean not to do that action immediately.

However, parents should use "No" judiciously. I have seen parents use the word *no* every time their child touches something, moves quickly, or, it seems, breathes too loudly. When parents say no too often, the child learns to tune them out, but when parents save their reprimands for the most important situations, the word *no* is more meaningful. An effective strategy is to catch them being good. Parents who can compliment their child during the moments of calm, or after a kind or gentle behavior, tend to raise better listeners. Their children are more likely to listen when a sporadic "No" is required. Experts agree that 10 positives for every 1 negative comment is an effective guideline when trying to teach kids to listen. Instead of automatically saying no, try to gently redirect or point your toddler in a more positive direction. For example, "Let's go play with our blocks instead of playing with the hair dryer. Hair dryers are for drying hair and blocks are for playing."

A toddler is more sophisticated than an infant, and as your child gets older, parenting requires more and more skill. Your toddler, like an infant, still has needs that should be reliably addressed; your toddler continues to depend on you for food and diaper changes. In some instances, your toddler can be involved in routines—doing things and not just having things done for her.

☑ Consistency Recommendations for Toddlers

- Toddlers require a great deal of attention. It's important to know where and what your toddler is doing at all times.
- As a parent, be consistent about boundaries.
    - Safety boundaries are very important for toddlers. For example, always use a car seat, hold hands in a parking lot, and use safety gates and outlet covers to avoid dangerous situations.
    - Establish rules of safety that your toddler will understand. "No biting." "No pulling hair." Be careful not to send inconsistent messages by allowing playful hair pulling, biting, or laughing. Laughing at a negative behavior will give children the impression that what they are doing is all right. Toddlers do not know the difference.
- Make sure "No" takes on an important meaning.
    - Follow-through is critical when emphasizing the importance of "No." Save the word *no* for dangerous and important situations (eg, putting a coin into his mouth). Say, "No, don't put that coin into your mouth." Then if your child does not immediately stop, take the coin away.

- As a parent, avoid overusing the word *no*. Whenever possible, try to gently redirect your toddler into positive behavior. Use the 10 positives for every 1 negative comment guideline.

- It is important to use routines in order to establish consistency. Gradually expand and add to the routines that were introduced during a child's infancy. For example, sleep routines can include activities such as baths, diaper changes, reading a story, singing the same lullaby, and implementing a set amount of cuddling before laying your child down to rest and saying, "Good night, we love you very much!"

- Toddlers will test parents because they are exploring and learning boundaries. Parents should maintain a consistently calm demeanor when responding to their toddler's misbehaviors. By parenting calmly, you teach your child to cope better with her own distress.

- When a toddler interrupts, parents can hold up a finger to signal that they will be right with her, and then they can respond to their child within 15 seconds. This will teach their child to wait.

- An active strategy to teach a toddler to wait is to have the toddler gently place her hand onto her parent's arm or hand to indicate that she wants something, but without interruption, as she is taught to stay quiet until her parent turns and looks toward her. Use praise to reinforce when your toddler does the right sequence of behaviors.

- Some appropriate "cause and effect" toys for toddlers at this age include hammer boxes, jack-in-the-box, and baby dolls with movable parts. Water and sand toys such as funnels, shovels, and buckets—for use in the tub or out in a sandbox—are also good.

- Musical toys are another great tool to teach cause and effect. Drums, maracas, tambourines, xylophones, or clapping to the music can be used to reinforce this concept and can help your toddler develop understanding of musical or auditory sequences.

Step 2: Introduce order

Learning to sequence is a building process that begins during infancy and continues through the teen years. All the strategies you have learned about in the previous chapter, Chapter 3, Raising an Organized Infant, should continue during the toddler years, but toddlers are capable of learning more-sophisticated lessons about order. Continue to support your toddler with routines for bedtime, feeding, and bathing. When your toddler is ready (ages 2–3½), start to introduce toileting routines. Parents can also increase the complexity of "cause and effect" toys and back-and-forth play. Turn taking is, in itself, a type of order; therefore, any activity (eg, building blocks with a parent, playing catch or chase games) during which a child can begin to learn "my turn, your turn" is an important lesson for teaching order at this age.

In addition to rapidly expanding mental capacity, your toddler gains the ability to move around and explore. One can watch a toddler rummage through a room full of toys like a dog in search of a bone, knocking over everything in his way and leaving destruction wherever he goes. Parents must learn to watch their toddlers closely because their behavior and actions seem random and chaotic. At this age, toddlers have an underdeveloped sense of order, and it is imperative not only to their learning, but also to their safety, that parents introduce their toddler to order. Parents can reinforce this teaching by setting clear and consistent limits.

Cause and Effect

During the toddler years, parents reinforce the 2-step sequence of cause and effect. The toys we give our toddlers, the way we respond to their behavior, and the things we say can all be important teaching skills. When your child does something right, the feedback you give reinforces the action. Positive feedback, such as telling your child, "Good job," when he puts his toy away, or brings you a new diaper during changing time, or allows you to wash his hair without complaining, is a cause and effect response that encourages positive behaviors. As a general rule, children should be supported with positives many more times than they are given negatives. As a parent, try and look for good behavior and "catch them being good."

Toddlers can use more-advanced cause and effect toys than infants. Take advantage of your child's ability to walk and give her toys that she can pull around the house. The classic jack-in-the-box is great for a toddler with the finger skills needed to turn the crank. Toddlers love pop-up toys that open when they push a button or turn a crank. Dolls that open and shut their eyes when you pick them up and lay them down are also good teaching tools. None of these toys require batteries. Use the classic cause and effect toys to introduce sequential order to your toddler.

Order of Language

Parents of toddlers can also introduce sequencing by exposing their child to the language of order. Parents should point out sequences by counting and emphasize beginnings and endings. Use the language of sequences. Words such as *first, second, next, end,* and *last* are important temporal (chronological) placeholders that 1- or 2-year-olds can begin to understand. As a parent, you can expose your toddler to these terms more than 20 times a day. When my children were younger, I often remember counting with them everywhere we went. I recall that the apartment we lived in had 13 steps, the first house we owned had 11 steps, and then we moved to another home that had only 2 steps. So, instead, we would count how many steps it would take us to walk up the steep driveway: 35.

After age 2, more-sophisticated time concepts can be introduced. Toddlers can associate words with activities that become placeholders for time. *Breakfast, lunch,* and *dinnertime; night* and *morning* times; and *bedtime* all suggest a conceptual order that a child can begin to understand. So talk to your child as you move throughout your day, and use these placeholders for time as a frame of reference, for example, "We can go to the park after lunchtime" or "We can brush our teeth after breakfast and dinnertime." When parents use these terms, toddlers are introduced to the concept of time, which will obviously be important for organization when they get older.

Order of Play

The toys we choose, the songs we sing, and the games we play can all support the concept of order. Offer toys that encourage steps, such as picking up a telephone and pretending to talk, performing simple puzzles, and building blocks. Expose your toddler to numbers by pointing out numbers and letters and by letting your child play with numbered blocks. Remember to reinforce the end of sequences by helping your toddler clean up before moving on to the next task, thereby introducing the concept of finished.

Parents should be reading and singing to toddlers every day. Many rhymes you sing and story tales you read emphasize order. Picture books that have the theme of sleeping (eg, *Goodnight Moon*) end with the character going to sleep. The songs we sing can also have order, such as the classic "Itsy Bitsy Spider," during which the spider goes up, comes down, and starts over again, and pat-a-cake, during which we prepare the treat before we put it into the oven: "First we pat it, then we roll it, and then we mark it with a B." Other songs involve counting, such as "5 Little Monkeys Jumping on the Bed." One of the family traditions I carried on from my Grandpa Jack was the use of "1 for the money, 2 for the show, 3 to get ready, and 4 to go!" to initiate fun activities. Order is everywhere, so be sure to take the time to point it out to your toddler, whenever you can.

 ## Sequencing Recommendations for Toddlers

Cause and Effect

- Setting limits emphasizes order by demonstrating cause and effect.
  - Encourage positive behavior.
  - Use the word *no* sparingly, but consistently, to safely guide your exploring toddler.

Teaching Order

- Whenever possible, introduce the idea that all tasks have a beginning, a middle, and an end.

- For instance, take out a toy, play with the toy, and then clean up the toy.
- Introduce turn taking to demonstrate order.
  - While stacking blocks, for instance, say out loud, "My turn, now your turn." Soon, the child will learn to anticipate what turn comes next.
- Expand back-and-forth and play.
  - Games such as peekaboo and "peep eye" that were introduced during infancy can evolve into rolling a ball back and forth and playing chase and tag.

Order of Play

- Introduce toys that require a sequence of steps to get an effect.
  - For young toddlers, these toys include hammering balls into a hole to initiate a chain of events and pulling a string to trigger spinning an arrow, which lands on a picture of an animal and initiates the appropriate animal sound.
- The same musical toys that were used to teach cause and effect can also be used to introduce sequences.
  - Music is, in itself, a sequence, so encourage toddlers to dance, clap, sing, and play along.
- Allow for ample "free exploration" time in the bathtub and a sandbox.
  - Let your child explore the results of building a sandcastle by shoveling sand into a pail. Or let her fill a small container with water in the tub.

Order of Language

- Parents should be *constantly* narrating life events to expose their child to the language of sequencing.
  - Introduce activities using words of order (eg, *first*, *second*, and *third*; *beginning*, *middle*, and *end*; and *ready*, *set*, *go*).
- Parents should seek opportunities to count out loud to their toddler (eg, when walking upstairs, when putting toys away, when cooking food).
- Your toddler will love to hear you sing songs and read stories that emphasize order (eg, *Chicka Chicka Boom Boom* and *The Very Hungry Caterpillar*).

Step 3: Give everything a place

Pay attention to how your toddler plays. Toddlers have the capacity to crawl, scoot, cruise, and walk—thereby increasing their capacity and speed for exploration. Toddlers are aware of their surroundings and appreciate spatial patterns. I remember that when our first child was 18 months old, he would run loops in our house; when excited, he would run from the kitchen to the dining room, from there to the family room, from there to the entrance hall, and from there back to our kitchen. We were in a new house when our second son was a toddler, and he created his own loop: kitchen to the living room, there to the family room, and there back to the kitchen. This dizzying display indicated that my toddlers had a spatial sense of their surroundings.

As a parent, you quickly become aware of how acute your toddler's vision has become as he finds every piece of lint, trash, or whatever else has fallen onto the floor. This is a sign that a toddler is ready to explore visual patterns. So, help him explore the world. Point out interesting clouds, the shadow formed by the sun passing through the leaves of a tree, or the wood grain on a table. Teach him to attend to what he sees.

It is amazing the amount of mess a toddler can make once he is able to move. Since a toddler's attention span is so short, he moves from one activity to the next leaving a trail of disaster in his wake. By the time you stop to clean up one mess, he has already made 2 more. Parents should in turn take desperate measures to secure the safety of their household. We block access to plugs with special covers that are even difficult for adults to remove, we put seemingly annoying locks onto our cabinets, we put up gates that we have to step over to go upstairs, and we also keep the door open when using the bathroom to keep surveillance on the "mini wrecking machine." But, of course, exploration by a toddler is a good thing—you should not try to stop it. There will be messes at home from now until he leaves to college. However, in time you will be able to teach your toddler to organize his chaos.

Location

By giving everything a place starting when children are young, parents strengthen these associations for their children. If we emphasize this principal early, someday, when they are old enough to clean their rooms, our children will know that even small objects such as a pencil and a sock have a place. For toddlers, spatial associations are based on the consistent location of objects and activities; for example, their high chair is for eating, Mom's rocking chair is for breastfeeding, the bed is for sleeping, and the diaper station is for getting their diaper changed. Be consistent in your use of these stations, and gradually add task-specific locations around the house. My wife and I had a very tiny apartment when our first child was born. We needed to make good use of the space. We had a playpen for our son to play with pop-up toys, the Johnny jumper was in the doorway to the kitchen, the rocker saucer was in the dining area, a play mat with soft and chewy toys was in the living room, and a bin of balls was in his bedroom. My wife and I would move him from one zone to the next when his enthusiasm began to wane. The point is that it was my child who moved from zone to zone and not the toys. When our toddler began to walk, I could ask him to go get a ball or his baby Ernie, and he would know exactly where to find them. Giving items a place helps establish spatial associations for your child; it is actually a learning lesson. A spatial association means that a child makes the mental connection between a thought, idea, or object and a location. I will discuss this more later, because this type of thinking becomes increasingly important when a child enters school and begins to read.

Size and Shape

Your toddler is at the age of understanding the concept of size and shape. He may not understand the word *big,* but he may recognize that a big ball cannot fit into a small hole. Reinforce this concept with your child using simple toys such as shape sorters, beginner puzzles, and blocks. Blocks can be stacked, but balls cannot, which teaches your toddler the idea that cubed objects are stackable. He will use the concept of size and shape as he begins to build more as a preschooler.

Spatial Language

Parents should teach spatial language concepts to toddlers. Words that describe location are much more difficult to learn than most nouns that describe a person, place, or thing. Location is an abstract concept, and it is confusing because its meaning is relative; for example, something next to you is not necessarily next to your toddler. You can demonstrate language concepts to your toddler through play around the house: "Daddy is under the table and Mommy is sitting on top of a ball." Use the word *where* to trigger your child to look for objects (eg, "Where is Mommy?" or "Where is Baby Bear?"). Begin to introduce the prepositions, such as *over* or *under,* that your toddler will better understand and master by the time he is 3 or 4.

Another way to teach your toddler is to build upon the understanding that objects exist even when they cannot be seen, by playing hiding games. Two-year-olds like to find things. When my children entered my room in the morning, I would hide under my blankets. If they did not notice the lump hiding under the blankets, I would squeak gradually louder until they located me. This game evolved to hiding around the house. I would hide and say, "Come and find me." I was building their scanning skills and would be rewarded with a big hug when I was captured; we both were winners.

Finally, parents should not mix up the need to teach how every-thing has a place with an obsessive need for cleanliness. It is important to remember that children should not be raised in a sterile environment; there will be disorder and disarray! Making a mess is an expected con-sequence of many natural developmental processes. Parents should not deprive their child of opportunities to learn and explore out of fear that their child will get dirty. I have met parents who spoon-fed their 3-year-old, out of fear that he would throw food onto the floor and get all messy, but, in doing so, they prevented their child from having the opportunity to explore the properties of food and to learn how to feed himself. Unintentionally, their child did not practice his fine motor control nor gain the confidence that comes with feeding oneself, a step toward independence. Children should be allowed to dig in the mud, splash in puddles, and, if they want to, dump out all their plastic bricks. However, when the play is done, parents need to support them in learning to put things away in the right place.

Spatial Skill Recommendations for Toddlers

Giving Everything a Place

- Continue to emphasize consistent locations for feeding, sleeping, and diaper changing.
- Designate several play stations or zones around the house where certain toys or activities are kept.
  - For instance, parents can assign a bin for stuffed animals, a shelf for puzzles and crafts, a spot for trains, a drawer in the kitchen for child-friendly plates and cups, and an area for physical play.
  - Establishing these domains when a child is young helps develop the association between a location and an activity and demonstrates to the child that everything has a place. As children grow older, the zones may change, but the concepts remain the same.
- Set a good example for your child by letting him observe you cleaning up and putting things away in a consistent place, and always encourage him to help you.

Spatial Awareness

- Play peekaboo games that encourage spatial recognition.
  - For instance, the "Where is...?" guessing game encourages your child to

look for the location of things around her. From behind a blanket, say, "Where is Daddy?" Lower the blanket, point to your child, and say, "Here I am!" Repeat this as long as your child is enjoying the game. The game can be varied by changing the subject, that is, using people or objects familiar to the toddler. Mommy, Daddy, a teddy bear, a sister, a brother, or other familiar people and your toddlers' toys can be used.

- Puzzles can help children recognize visual spatial patterns.

■ Introduce the simplest puzzles such as shape sorters (eg, put a circle into the round hole and a square into the square space). Next, have your child work with pieces that are large and easy to manipulate, such as wooden or plastic puzzles that are easy to handle.

■ Encourage visual attention to the specifics of everyday items, which helps develop a habit of vigilance to future details such as math signs and letters within words.

- Parents can call attention to interesting patterns in the world around them, such as the scenery on a long drive, the mineral patterns in a rock, the shapes found in the clouds, or the features of a pet's fur.

Eye-Hand Coordination

■ Provide toys that can be pushed (shopping cart) or pulled (dog on wheels) around the house to encourage spatial exploration.

■ To promote visual-motor planning (eye-hand coordination), introduce your child to "balloon bop"—encouraging your toddler to keep an inflated balloon aloft by bopping it up as it repeatedly gently falls to the ground. Children love this game, and it can be played by themselves or family members can play too.

■ Children can also practice throwing and catching toys such as large beach balls, bandanas or handkerchiefs, lightweight foam balls, or beanbags. These activities can help your toddler develop eye-hand coordination.

Step 4: Practice forward thinking

A toddler, like an infant, continues to lack the cognitive capacity (the brain of a toddler, like an infant, is not yet mature enough to perform forward thinking) for sophisticated forward thinking. Stranger anxiety is a good example of limited forethought (the ability to predict what will happen next). Stranger anxiety peeks during the toddler years, because in the mind of a child who has not yet matured, there develops a fear that when Mom leaves the toddler's sight, she will be gone forever. Not yet can the toddler use hindsight (the ability to consider past experiences) to remember that Mom has returned every other time she went away. However, with consistent opportunities, the toddler becomes familiar with his mother's departure and gradually overcomes this fear.

Glimmers of foresight are exhibited in toddlers when parents are consistent with routines. At this age, children can learn routines and start to anticipate the next step. For example, a parent might say to a 2-year-old, "Let's go to the park!" If they have an established routine, the child may run and get his sneakers. The child may be making the connection that to play at the park he will need those shoes. Likewise, "Let's go take a bath" may prompt your child to remove her clothes, because she knows that bathing requires nakedness. A parent can encourage her toddler to think ahead by asking questions instead of delivering instructions. The parent can say, "We are going to the park, so what should we bring?" to prompt the child to think ahead. Toddlers can anticipate the next step, but they may not generate original thought when using foresight. Remember, consistent parenting and the use of routines help solidify in a child's mind what things go together, and this readies the child to think ahead.

Step 5: Promote problem-solving

Most problem-solving skills remain elusive throughout the toddler years. They are not grasping the big picture, their insight is limited, and they do not yet take the perspective of others. Still, they begin to show signs of cognitive flexibility (the mental ability to switch between 2 different concepts or ideas) when figuring out how to get what they want. A toddler, for example, might push a light coffee table against a wall in order to use it as a step to reach an object placed out of reach by a parent on the fireplace mantle. So, while you may feel frustrated that your child did not listen to you, pause and recognize what a cognitive accomplishment your child has made by figuring out how to get what he wants. Redirect, but do not scold, the creative kid.

Toddlers learn by exploration and experimentation. Finding a small object, placing it into their mouth, and then spitting it out—because of a parent's sharp warning to stop—is a learning process. An infant may learn the parent's intended lesson, to not put small objects into her mouth, or a possibly clever child may attempt the same act but, this time, when the parent is not looking. The child has considered at least one alternative option before tackling the issue. In the spirit of safety, it is easy to stifle your child's exploration by constantly watching over and directing everything your child does. But parents should balance the desire to keep a child safe with the need for a child to learn and explore. Try not to anticipate and solve all the needs of your child. Allow him the opportunity to struggle and get frustrated with a task. Watch him try to figure out how to obtain things that are out of his reach, are too heavy to move, or do not fit inside his grasp.

Toddlers show emerging abilities to imagine and pretend, which is important because pretending is an excellent way to practice solving problems. It is difficult to know how much an infant or a toddler remembers, but the general consensus is that they recall, at least subconsciously, much of what they see, hear, and feel. At around 15 months old, an organized toddler begins to reenact memories in her imitative play and later in her pretend play. Your child might, for instance, pick up a telephone and pretend to talk, try to push the vacuum, or sit in the front seat of a car and imitate steering. By age 2, children typically participate in symbolic play; for example, they could use a banana or a shoe to represent a telephone or a doll to represent a baby. When using a doll, your 2-year-old can reenact the hugs and kisses that you gave to her. Parents should promote imitative play and then once their child demonstrates competence, encourage her to pretend by suggesting variations to the play. For instance, if your child is stirring a pot, suggest an alternative such as making a cake. Or, better yet, ask her what she is making and then inquire about what else she might be able to create. Toddlers should be master explorers of their environment and also their minds; by parents providing new pretend scenarios, toddlers can explore their physical environment, language skills, and imagination.

Most 2-year-olds are impatient. Whatever they want, they want immediately. As parents, we have the instinct to help our children. There is, however, a trade-off when parents are indulgent. On the one hand, their offering may be a demonstration of love, but on the other hand, doing so prevents an opportunity for children to learn. Teaching a child to delay gratification encourages perspective taking. Explain that "Mommy cannot pick you up right now because she is on the telephone" or "Daddy cannot get you a cookie when he is on the toilet." Try not to say, "I will do it in a minute," unless, of course, you will actually do it in a minute. You do not want to reinforce delaying gratification while shattering his already delicate concept of time. By making your child wait briefly, you are also giving him the opportunity to practice dealing with his own boredom by flexibly considering other possibilities. Believe me, you will appreciate any flexible thinking that has emerged in your child as he enters the "terrible" twos, threes, and fours, and he will still love you even though you made him wait.

✓ Recommendations to Teach Problem-solving to Toddlers

Imagination

- Fifteen-month-olds can perform imitative play, so encourage creativity, imagination, and play.
- Once your child is imitating in his play, engage in simple role-playing. For instance, by pretending to be a lion, doctor, or fisherman, your child is learning to pretend and perform higher-order thinking and to pretend to think like someone or something else.

Exploration

■ Give your child the opportunity to think for himself. Set appropriate boundaries, but give your child the opportunities to explore, learn, and entertain himself. Try not to anticipate his needs. When he is stuck or frustrated, encourage him to request assistance.

■ Before your child is the age of 2, give your child crayons, washable pens, and chalk to make lines and squiggles on paper or the sidewalks. Soon after, she can try a simple coloring book with familiar objects to color, such as shapes and animals. Young children also love to paint. Be sure to compliment your child's creativity and make an effort to display her art.

■ Encourage the use of play dough so that your toddler can try to create simple items (eg, a cake, a flower, a snake, a bear).

■ Use the sandbox and bath time to develop budding science skills. Provide cups, funnels, and buckets, and demonstrate transferring the sand or bathwater from one item to the next.

Problem-solving

■ Gradually encourage children to make decisions for themselves. Instead of asking your young child "yes or no" questions, encourage your child to make a choice, for example, "Do you want to drink milk or water?" Older children can be asked open-ended questions such as "What do you want to drink?"

■ Teach toddlers to delay gratification. Learning to wait allows them to practice dealing with boredom while thinking about options and alternatives.

Perspective Taking

■ Begin to train your child to take perspective by using humor. Be silly to make him laugh, and encourage him to make you chuckle.

■ Eye contact is important for taking perspective. Look at your child's eyes while you speak, and encourage him to do the same.

Chapter 5

Raising an Organized Preschooler: The Years of Great Brain Growth

Preschool refers to children between the ages of 3 years and 5 years. During this period, children begin to recognize that they have a voice and can assert themselves. In actuality, the "terrible" twos happens between the ages of 2½ and 4, so preschoolers will challenge parents to step up their "parenting game." As your child asserts her newly found independence, she will, from time to time, have meltdowns and tantrums. These meltdowns occur because her ability to take other people's perspectives and her language-processing skills are immature. Although this can lead to difficult confrontations, and a lot of frustration, as a parent you should understand that it is an important part of her development. A child who makes healthy progress through this developmental stage should exit as a 5-year-old feeling competent and relatively independent.

While preschoolers may seek independence and competence, their judgement is still limited. They are just beginning to process and apply knowledge, to analyze and reason, and to evaluate and decide. As a result, they need to be protected from the dangers of the world. It is our job as parents to support independence while protecting our children from themselves. For example, while shopping in the mall, my 4-year-old used to like to wander and explore but would occasionally wander too far and lose track of me. I could have held his hand tightly and stifled his exploration or shamed him for wandering off, but instead, I let him wander and watched him very, very closely. As he explored, gaining self-confidence and independence, he eventually learned to look back to check in with me. He experienced brief moments of anxiety when he did not immediately see me, and this worry taught him to check in more often. When a child can learn a lesson on his own, he retains it much better than when it is verbally taught to him.

As your child grows, you will be impressed by all the clever things your preschooler does. This is because 4- and 5-year-olds are learning routines and demonstrating forward and backward thinking. They begin to use hindsight to learn from their experiences and foresight to anticipate outcomes. They will use their forward-thinking skills to do things that are funny in order to make you laugh, and sometimes they will use those same skills to make you mad. Most of all, you should notice how creative your child can be. Imagination and pretending should be a major component of her play. Preschoolers commonly develop imaginary friends, which allows them to think through situations from another perspective. At this age, my son had a pretend friend, Mary Ashley, who seemed to follow us everywhere. It was amazing to see how considerate my 4-year-old could be for this friend, for example, "Mom, Mary Ashley wants some ice cream too." Whenever possible, encourage imagination in your child because pretend play is one of the best ways to practice perspective taking, forward thinking, and problem-solving.

Step 1: Be consistent

Setting consistent expectations and following through with them is one of the most difficult parenting tasks, because there can be many variables to consider (eg, "We play with a balloon, but not a ball, in the house"), but children do not detect the subtleties of each circumstance. If, for example, a parent says yes to a child, who asks to play a game on the parent's phone while waiting for a table at a restaurant, then whenever he is bored, the child will ask for the phone. Similarly, if a child is permitted to stay up past bedtime to watch a television show, or is granted watching television during dinner, or is allowed to play fight with his father while getting ready for bed, he will ultimately ask for more. So, consistency is important. It is not that parents need to always say no, but when a child does stray from a set expectation, it should be clearly expressed to the child why this time is an exception. For instance, "You can have my phone to play a game this time because they said it will be 30 minutes before our table is ready and that is a very long time" or "You can stay up late tonight because we have friends visiting and this is a special circumstance." As children grow older, the circumstances become increasingly complex, but if parents establish rules, and understand the reasons behind the rules, it is possible to be both consistent and flexible at the same time.

Consistent parenting can support positive child behavior. Meltdowns are common among preschoolers when they do not get their way. Tantrums are normal during this phase of development, but their frequency can be reduced by using consistent schedules and routines. Preschoolers are pretty unskilled at anticipating, and so things do not always turn out the way they expect. Their unmet expectations such as losing a game or not getting to go first can result in a tantrum. Do not fear their upsets, but also do not give into them. As a parent, the last thing you want to do is reinforce to your child that a tantrum or a meltdown will get your child what she wants. Instead, be patient and calm and try to redirect or distract your child. Your child might need to take a time-out. For example, if your child decides to implode in aisle 5 of the grocery store, ask the checker to place your cart into the refrigerator while you take your child to the car to finish the upset. Don't worry, because yours is not the first child to melt down and grocery stores are familiar with this procedure.

As you know, 3- and 4-year-olds can move very quickly. A 4-year-old can elude the grasp of your hand, run down the driveway, and run into a street in seconds. Preschoolers' mobility requires vigilant parenting in order to keep them safe. While it is important to hold their hand in a parking lot, it is not realistic to hold on to them all day long, even though you might want to. It's more important as a parent to teach them the critical rules of safety. Parents can send this message in several ways: Parents can provide advance warning such as "Daddy is going to be opening the oven, so do not come close—it is very hot!" or "Let a dog sniff your hand before you pet it." Parents can use a stern voice such as "Do not run into the street." Parents can use a physical cue that comes naturally such as grabbing their child's hand in a busy parking lot or when a strange dog approaches. Most important, parents should consistently reinforce these messages so that children better recognize the importance of dangerous situations. Children learn these rules when parents teach the message consistently and frequently. Preschoolers are fragile. They move at great speed, but get hurt easily, and they melt down when things do not go their way. By being consistent, parents can help reduce difficult and dangerous behaviors.

☑ Consistency Recommendations for Preschoolers

- Boundaries and limits need to be clearly defined for young children. Parents need to
  - Clearly state and enforce rules (eg, no hitting, no running from a parent in a public place, no throwing food).
  - Set clear and consistent limits regarding critical safety boundaries so that your children understand (eg, always hold hands in parking lots; don't touch the hot stove; in crowded places, always stay an arm's length away from Mom and Dad).
- Balance limit setting with a child's need to explore.
  - It is important to set limits, but be careful, because saying no to everything tends to de-emphasize the importance of the most critical boundaries.
  - Do not fear your child's loud-crying meltdowns. Having meltdowns is a normal part of preschooler development as they continue to learn and assert their independence.
  - Set limits in public places the same way you would at home. Changing your standards in public places sends an inconsistent message to your child.

- Routines should be used to emphasize consistency. Solidify morning, mealtime, and breakfast routines.
- Reinforce consistent placement of objects.
  - Support cleaning up after a project.
  - Patiently encourage your child to play with just one toy at a time and to put the toy away before taking out the next object.
- Parents need to set consistent expectations.
  - Consistent follow-through from a parent will become increasingly important when teaching time (eg, 5 more minutes) and when it comes to location (eg, child takes off shoes and puts them into the closet when arriving home).
  - Do not give multiple warnings, even if your child gets upset. After time, she will come to understand what warnings such as "5 more minutes" mean. Multiple warnings are a form of inconsistency.
  - Parents must also provide a consistent emotional response. Keep the level of upset proportionate to the infraction, injury, or situation.

Step 2: Introduce order

During the preschool years, your child will demonstrate tremendous growth in language, imagination, and understanding of concepts, and this helps enables him to acquire a much greater sequential awareness (understanding of order). Between the ages of 3 and 4, a child's ability to understand conceptual language is emerging and so parents can challenge their child with new sequencing vocabulary. By age 4, your child should have a good grasp of prepositional time concepts (eg, after, before, during, next) and an emerging understanding of complex time concepts such as yesterday, today, and tomorrow. Parents can reinforce time by pairing a visual with a time concept, such as showing tomorrow by pointing it out on a calendar or showing 5 minutes by showing the hands of a clock. The more a child can relate to time with personal experience, the easier it will be to learn. So, for instance, counting to 60 while tying shoes or setting a timer for 2 minutes while brushing teeth reinforces units of time. Times of transition can be important for teaching time. By using finite statements such as "We will be leaving in 5 minutes," parents demonstrate that time interval. Of course, it is very important to remember that this only works if parents consistently follow through in 5 minutes. As parents, we have all been in that situation of having many things to do, and it's easy to say, "OK, in 5 minutes," and that becomes 10 minutes and then 15 minutes. In fact, it is just as easy to stunt a child's emerging concept of time, by not following through with a time restriction, as it is to build her sense of order.

Order of Language

Did you know that the language we expose our children to can have order? Stories and jokes have an order to them and are excellent practice tools for young children. Many beginner books begin ("Once upon a time") and finish ("The end") using the same type of format. This teaches beginning readers and story listeners that there is an order—a beginning, a middle, and an end—to each story we read. Your preschooler may not automatically recognize the order of a written or spoken story, but you can help show the structure by emphasizing order in your delivery. Look for opportunities during the day for your child to tell short stories. Encourage him to learn and tell the simple stories such as *The Three Little Pigs* and *Goldilocks and the Three Bears* so that he can practice sequencing (remembering the order of each story). Kids love to tell stories, and you know they have learned an important lesson when they begin it with "Once upon a time," followed by "The end."

Jokes are another early exposure to sequences, and most little children love to tell jokes and giggle. Children often make up their own jokes. A young client of mine once used this one: "Knock, knock," and after I answered, "Who is there?" he said, "Knocking over my glass of water," and then he knocked the glass over, laughing hysterically. You will often find that your child's jokes may not be very funny to you, but, nevertheless, you should still encourage the comical experimentation. Knowing that a joke has a setup and a punch line shows that your child is beginning to understand the sequence of being witty.

Parents should expose their child to numbers and counting, because preschoolers can learn these skills. At first, children begin reciting numbers in order, and shortly after that, they develop one-to-one correspondence, meaning they can count objects, not just recite them. Just like you did with your toddler, continue to integrate counting into your daily activities. Numbers make great conversation starters with preschoolers, such as "How many apples are on the table?" or "How many chicken nuggets did you eat?" Four-year-olds understand simple number concepts, so ask them, "Which group has more or less?" These repetitive questions will help them build strong number skills.

A preschooler may not yet be ready to tell time, but you can introduce preschoolers to clocks by reminding them that it is bedtime when the hand on the clock points to the 8 or when the digital clock reads "7, 3, 0." I remember that when my 3-year-old daughter wanted to know how many days there were before an event, she would ask in her adorable, squeaky little voice, "How many more sleeps?" She didn't quite understand words such as *tomorrow* or *days,* but she was developing her sense of time according to her sleep cycle. And, in time, your child will learn this too.

Teaching Order

Show your preschool-aged child that tasks can be broken down into steps. For example, when it comes time to clean his room, explain to him that "First, we pick up clothes; second, we put our stuffed animals away; and third, we clean up all of the Legos from the floor." Another way to emphasize sequences is to put order to the day. For instance, when you are running around doing errands, you can point out the order, such as "First, we are going to the dry cleaner; next, we will pick up your sister from dance lessons; and finally, we are going to the grocery store." Remember that although many children at age 4 can remember 3 or more steps, not every child can. Sometimes it helps to write down the steps, and, since most preschoolers cannot read, start with picture schedules (see Appendix B, Creating Mini Routines) that list out the sequence of steps needed to complete a task.

Implementing Routines

Routines. Routines. Routines. Routines make us more efficient, and familiarity and repetition are soothing to most people. At every age, even my age, it is important to continue physiological routines for sleeping, eating, and going to the bathroom. Parents of preschoolers can now begin to introduce a number of subtler routines. Many parents may not think of getting dressed, eating breakfast, and leaving the house as routines, but effective parents develop rituals around these activities and times of transition. Parents can create picture lists, if needed, for each of these important transitions. These simple sequences foreshadow the more complicated routines (eg, getting themselves ready for school, doing homework, writing essays) that they will someday need to master. See Box 5-1 for more routines.

Box 5-1

Common Routines for Preschoolers That Can Be Routinized

■ Using the bathroom   ■ Leaving the house

■ Getting dressed   ■ Getting into the car

■ Preparing for bed   ■ Arriving home

■ Eating meals

Order of Play

The emergence of imaginative play competencies creates the opportunity to practice routines. Children can pretend to cook, be a teacher, or get a doll ready for bed. Each of these scenarios involves steps. Encourage your child to go through each step, and when she misses a step, jokingly point it out, for example, "Wait a minute. Are you putting your doll to bed naked? The baby can't be naked, because she will wet the bed." These reminders can be fun, and they also cue your child that the sequence is incomplete. Playtime allows parents to give positive attention and spend time with their child. Parents should balance the need to model the order in play with their child's need for creative expression. Since just about every task a child does involves steps, helping the child understand that these steps are consistent and predictable is important.

A fun way to teach sequences is by playing games. Remember, just the act of taking out, playing, and putting away a game is a sequence. In addition, there are many fun games for children that involve turn taking and order. Most simple games, such as Chutes and Ladders, Candy Land, and Trouble, promote turn taking and counting. I like to make up games with my children that involve following directions. Sometimes I used to pretend and send them on a top secret mission, with "Go to the laundry room, find a sock, and then hide it in a blue book in the bookcase." Children are motivated by creativity and laughter, so a clever parent can fold some education into the creative play.

✓ Sequencing Recommendations for Preschoolers

Language of Order

- Expand the use of language to emphasize order. When speaking, use temporal and numerical place keepers such as
    - *First, second,* and *third*
    - *In the beginning, then,* and *finally*
    - *To begin with, after that,* and *in conclusion*
    - *Your turn* and *then my turn*
    - *First this, next this,* and *then that*
- Count to demonstrate one-to-one correspondence. For example, count out loud every time you walk upstairs or downstairs.
- Introduce counting concepts (eg, "How many apples did we buy?") and games that introduce counting and relative value concepts (eg, "Which is

more or less?"). Grocery shopping trips are a perfect time to ask your child these questions. "Which one is cheaper?"

■ Counting can also be used to show that numbers can represent time. Parents, for instance, can time their child by counting out loud as she races to find her shoes.

■ Introduce the math terms *plus* and *minus*. Encourage your child to use his fingers to figure out, for instance, what happens if a person has 3 apples and then gets 2 more apples.

■ Give preschoolers a chance to follow directions when doing everyday activities, such as helping with baking from a recipe or preparing a meal by adhering to directions on a package.

■ When telling stories and jokes, emphasize the order that is inherent in these activities.

Teaching Time

■ Use time limits to introduce your child to units of time and time concepts (eg, later, soon, before, after, tomorrow, yesterday). Try and teach these concepts throughout your day with your child. On your drive in the car to preschool, you can say to your child, "After school today, we are going to stop at the post office," or "Tomorrow we are going to go the park with Grandma." These little, constant examples will help your child understand these units of time.

■ It is also important for your child to learn time expectations (eg, 5 minutes, 10 minutes, 30 minutes). As parents, we have all been in that situation when your child starts to cry when it's time to leave the park. A helpful way to teach your child time expectations is by giving her a warning before it's time to leave. You can say, "We will be leaving the park in 10 minutes, so go do your favorite thing 1 more time before we leave." It's an easier transition for kids if they realize this small window of time allows them to do 1 more thing. Some parents even set a timer on their phone so that their kids can see they have 5 minutes, and when the alarm goes off, they know it's time to leave. Remember, it is critical that you are consistent with follow-through. Five minutes should always mean 5 minutes.

■ Setting a standard time of day for bedtimes and mealtimes, whenever possible, should be consistently followed. Providing little reminders to your children that bedtime is in 20 minutes will help them with this important understanding.

Implementing Routines

■ Encourage simple household routines for common activities: dressing, getting ready for bed, going on a car ride, and leaving a playdate, for example. If your child has difficulty remembering or transitioning from one step to the next, create mini routines using picture cards to help show order and expectations. (See Appendix B, Creating Mini Routines.)

■ Mini routines are an intermediate step between parental coaching and independence. These routines should be no more than 5 steps each, and they should be displayed in a prominent location where they cannot be overlooked by the child. Picture lists can be particularly useful for young children or children on the autism spectrum. (See Appendix B, Creating Mini Routines.)

■ Use "backward chaining" to gradually teach a child a new skill or routine. With this technique, parents, at first, perform all the steps needed to complete a project except for the last one, which the child completes on her own (or is taught to complete on her own). As she becomes successful with the last step, guide her through all but the last 2 steps, and so on, until the child is able to sequence the entire behavior independently. Dressing and cleaning up a room are excellent examples of when backward chaining can be introduced to a preschool-aged child.

Teaching Order

■ Emphasize that every project has a beginning, a middle, and an end. Remind preschoolers about finishing one task before moving on to the next; for example, make sure they flush the toilet, cap the toothpaste, and clear their plate from the table.

Order of Play

■ Play games that involve turn taking.

Don't be a "do it for them" parent.

One pitfall of raising a child who lacks organization is that when the child struggles to get ready, parents do things for her, either out of concern or to simply move the child through the day's activities. To get children ready for the first day of kindergarten, parents wake the child, lay out her clothes, make her breakfast, and check to see that she has her backpack. If parents are still doing all these things for the child 2 years later, when that child is in second grade, there may be a problem with either the child's organization or the parent's ability to let go. The parent's efforts to get the child out the door may unintentionally prevent the child from developing her own sense of organization, by depriving the child the opportunity to exercise her sequential working memory.

Step 3: Give everything a place

A preschool-aged child experiences tremendous growth in language development, but spatial development happens more gradually. While the visual cortex, the part of the brain that processes sensory information from the eyes, is still young and developing, your preschooler's memory is becoming increasingly effective. Your child has an emerging understanding of routines and the capacity to remember visual associations (such as the letters of the alphabet). This is an age at which she begins to understand the concept of cleanup and develops the capacity to throw and catch moving objects. Our job as parents is to promote the development of these skills.

Location

The memory system becomes increasingly effective during the preschool period. Preschoolers make associations so quickly that most parents begin to think they must have the smartest child in the world; preschoolers learn, whether we teach them or not. The problem is that if we don't teach them, they may not learn the most important things. When it comes to spatial awareness, it is important to reinforce the concepts of location, shape, and visually paired associations. Continue to show your child that everything has a place. You can begin to get more specific with your spatial routines, by giving *specific* items a place. Just as you have a place in your kitchen for forks, spoons, and knives (which by now your child has learned), your child is capable of learning that there is a place for her shoes, her toothbrush, her "big kid" underpants, and her favorite shampoo.

As these places for your child's things are established, your child should be encouraged to clean up after herself. But remember that cleaning up is more complicated than it seems. Cleaning up requires a plan, and at first, parents may need to support this task by providing a structure or a list of items to put away. While it is true that the original location of the toys (eg, stored in the closet) remains the same, many variables influence cleaning up. By the time a child has finished playing, there are usually many toys mixed together all over the floor. Although it seems obvious that a child should chunk, or group, like toys together to make this task simpler, some children do not make this calculation and will need help. It is unrealistic to expect that your preschool-aged child will consistently remember on his own to put things where they go, but with your consistent prompting (eg, "Remember to put your shoes where they go") and by breaking down the task (eg, "Let's find all the blocks and put them away first"), he should be able to remember.

Spatial Language

During this period, your preschooler will acquire a vocabulary of tens of thousands of words. He will understand pronouns and prepositions. Parents can use the child's language growth to teach spatial awareness. Talk to your child using prepositions of location, for example, "Please bring me your socks, which are sitting on top of the laundry basket." By age 5, most children are familiar with the most common prepositions (Box 5-2). You can also use words to play location games with your child that require giving verbal instructions, such as "Put the ball behind the table," "Place the ball between us but closer to you," or "Set the ball next to the table." Your child's language development is a wonderful tool to use when teaching spatial awareness.

Box 5-2

Prepositions That Are Commonly Used to Show Location or Direction

Above	Between	Next	Outside of
Ahead of	By	Next to	Over
Apart from	Down	On	Through
Around	In	Onto	Under
Behind	Inside	Out	Underneath
Below	Inside of	Out from	
Beneath	Into	Out of	
Beside	Near to	Outside	

Now that your child has language and memory, he can learn the names of objects. I subscribe to a method of naturalistic teaching when it comes to shapes, numbers, and letters of the alphabet. I believe that for preschool-aged children, acquisition of this knowledge should occur through play and not from flash cards. Instead of dedicating 30 minutes a day to teach your child his numbers, shapes, and letters, look for opportunities to teach throughout the day. For example, when driving, see whether your child can find any circles, squares, or hexagons; when reading to your child, ask her to point out a particular letter when she sees it; and go on a number hunt in the grocery store. Make learning fun and enjoyable, and she will want to do it the rest of her life. Your preschooler should be playing with puzzles, and you should gradually increase the difficulty as your child's ability grows. Give your child number blocks and foam letters so that he can create his own made-up words. Read alphabet books that associate pictures and sounds with letters of the alphabet. Select counting books that teach one-to-one correspondence. Lessons are everywhere, and learning can be fun if a parent or a grandparent is tuned into teaching.

Spatial Toys

Continuing with this concept of teaching through play, the toys and games we chose to play with our children should have a spatial component to help develop spatial awareness. The first example of toys that build spatial awareness is construction toys such as trains and blocks. As your preschooler gets closer to school age, the building toys will evolve to include Lincoln Logs, Lego bricks, K'nex sets, Zoob sets, and Connectagons. Building develops a sense of spatial relations as well as promotes eye-hand coordination. Take advantage of your preschooler's growing imagination and encourage her to build with a purpose and not just stack. By you asking, "What are you making?" or "What should we build?" she may begin to build with a plan. Don't forget about hide-and-seek, which for a parent finally gets to be fun because a preschooler will put some effort into hiding and not just stand behind the curtain every time. You can also hide objects, such as a penny, and give clues (eg, "You're getting warmer, or colder") to help your child with systematic visual scanning (to help your child learn to efficiently, quickly, and actively look for information or objects in her environment).

Artwork is another great opportunity for spatial exploration. Give your child opportunities to draw, paint, use glue, and sculpt with play dough. Do not worry about the inevitable mess that will be made from these activities. Just make sure you have a designated space in your house for art projects, so that art does not move to your walls, your floors, or your new sofa.

Ball play highlights a unique aspect of spatial processing. With ball play, the object moves relative to the child. In that regard, the child's brain is required to continuously calculate the location of objects. Consider the mental calculations that are required in order for a child to catch a ball. The brain must calculate both the rate of movement and the arc of travel in order to announce to the hands how fast they must move and at what spot the hands should be at so that the child will be prepared to catch, when the ball arrives. Calculus is needed to perform this equation on paper, but the preschool brain is beginning to perform the function. By the time a child goes to kindergarten at age 5, he should be able to catch a large ball thrown to him. Start by rolling balls back and forth, which reduces the complexity of the task, or by using balloons or beach balls that fall more slowly. Teach your child to play catch with, kick, throw, and hit a ball; these skills help develop the visual cortex. For any parents who are not very sporty, remember that teaching ball skills is like calculus for the visual cortex. You want your child to practice and have mastered these types of mental manipulations long before it comes time for him to drive a car.

Preschool-aged children have an incessant zest for life. They want to explore and learn and play all day long. Make learning fun for your children and there will be infinite opportunities for you to teach spatial awareness.

✔ Spatial Skill Recommendations for Preschoolers

Giving Everything a Place

- Continue to give everything a place, and make it obvious where things are kept in your house. It is not necessary to be obsessed with neatness: preschoolers are messy. The goal is to reinforce through repetition that everything has a consistent location.

- Do establish an organized filing system for toys. Do not simply throw everything into a toy box. Your child will not ever be able to find things or learn where things go. Instead, use bins (preferably clear) to store toys. For instance, there could be a bin designated for Lego bricks and another for toy cars.

- Since most preschoolers do know where things go, but lack the attention needed to remember to put things away, you should introduce routine cleanup times throughout the day, such as before meals and before going to bed. Cleanup can be mostly parent led, but the child can head up a portion of the cleaning project. For example, say, "You pick up the blocks, while I clean up these things," which will probably mean just about everything else, "and, if I finish before you, I can help you too."

Spatial Language

- Frequently use prepositions and language of location and direction (eg, *above, below, near, under*) when speaking with your preschool-aged child.

- Parents can point out geometric shapes in the real world: tires are circles, a stop sign is an octagon, a yield sign is a triangle, and tables are rectangles, for example.

- Select books that have letters and numbers that are tied to pictures so that the child can make word associations.

Spatial Games

- Puzzles are the most typical spatial games used by preschoolers. Puzzles introduce relative shape and size. Beginner puzzles require placing an object into a similarly shaped opening. More-advanced puzzles require connecting a dozen pieces to form a picture. By the time a child is ready for kindergarten, he may be capable of completing 24- to 48-piece puzzles. Be sure to use puzzles that are at your child's level; otherwise, he will become either bored or frustrated.

- Many games encourage spatial awareness. For example, to build the concept of left and right discrimination, the game Simon Says might be played (eg, "Simon says, 'Touch your left knee with your right hand,'" "Simon Says, 'Jump with your left foot'"). Another example is the "mirror game" during which students work in pairs facing each other, one student leads by generating movements, and the other mirrors the movements so that the students are doing the same thing at the same time. The idea is not to throw off your partner, but to move at the same time, that is, to be a mirror image. This activity promotes body awareness, balance and coordination, spatial awareness, and motor control. With practice, children can perfect more and more complex series of movements.

■ A great game to observe how your child develops the concept of spatial awareness is to play hide-and-seek. Beginning players hide out in the open, with no sense that if they can see you, you can also see them. More-sophisticated hiders may settle behind an object, such as an ottoman or a curtain, unaware that a part of them obviously sticks out. Eventually, the child learns to hide in cabinets or under beds where it would be more difficult for an adult to find him.

■ "Something's missing" is a game that helps develop spatial memory. A group of objects can be placed onto a table. When the child is not looking, 1 or 2 items can be removed and the child is then required to identify the missing object. More objects can be added as the memory improves.

■ To promote visual-motor planning and eye-hand coordination, begin practice throwing and catching balls. Since most preschool students are new to catching, it would be dangerous to start by throwing a ball at them from a distance. Instead, begin by rolling balls back and forth to give the child a sense of 2-dimensional movement. To introduce 3-dimensional tracking, use a slow-falling object, such as a balloon or beach ball, and have the child try to keep it in the air by hitting it each time it falls. Once these tasks are mastered, progress to playing catch with soft balls and with beanbags.

Step 4: Practice forward thinking

Preschool is the age when foresight and hindsight take hold and children begin to grow the capacity to think ahead. When your 4-year-old sneakily takes a cookie off the counter, he is thinking forward about the consequences of getting caught, or when your 5-year-old makes up a story about how red marker ended up on the walls of the kitchen, she is thinking about potential problems of telling the truth. I chose these negative examples to emphasize that kids are learning, and what looks like a lie or stealing may be a child with low impulse control and the emerging ability to plan ahead. More often than not, forward thinking is a positive undertaking, such as grabbing a coat before leaving the house or remembering to bring along a book on a busy day of errands with Mom.

A simple measure of forward thinking is called the **Tower Test.** Children are given a mixed-up tower puzzle and then are shown the completed product. Then the child is given the tower with rings in a mixed-up order and asked to rearrange the rings in as few steps as possible by removing and replacing sets of rings. During this task, 4-year-olds could anticipate 1 step and 5-year-olds could plan out a few steps needed to solve a puzzle.[10] Similarly, in an experiment asking children to plan out efficient routes through a zoo, 5 years was the age when children started having success with this assignment. By the end of the preschool period, children are developmentally ready to use forward thinking, and like any skill, to be actualized it needs to be practiced.[28]

Modeling Forward Thinking

As parents, we are constantly forward thinking as we plan our schedules, our routes, what we say, and how we act. Children learn by watching us, so it can be useful if parents can be transparent with their thoughts so that they can model this behavior for their children. Talk about plans with your child so that he can see what goes into getting from one place to the next. Discuss getting ready and time management. For example, if your child asks whether he can watch a television show, you might ask, "How long is the show, because we are leaving the house in 45 minutes." If you learn that the show is 30 minutes long, you might want to ask how much time it will take for him to get ready to go and suggest that he get ready *before* he watches the show. In this example, you demonstrated your planning and made him part of the process.

Your child is developing his ability to think forward, but this is difficult and his thinking may be incomplete. Before a child is age 5, the key is to emphasize the importance of a plan. Begin to break down tasks for your preschool child. Demonstrate, for instance, how getting ready for bed can be done in steps (eg, brush teeth, use bathroom, wash hands and face, and put on pajamas). If your child is having problems learning this, use picture schedules (see Appendix B, Creating Mini Routines) to show your child the steps. You can help this process with conversation. Together, you and your child can co-construct a shared vision of a future event. The following conversation is an example of a forward-thinking conversation with a 4-year-old child:

Father: Today, we are going to the beach.

Child: Can we play in the water?

Father: Yes, but the water is going to be cold.

Child: We can use a wet suit.

Father: What else do we need?

Child: A towel.

Father: Good idea, so how about toys to play with?

Child: We could bring a shovel and a bucket. Will Carly go too?

Father: We had fun last time with Carly, so I can ask her mom if she can come with us.

Child: OK.

Father: I am going to get a bag and suntan lotion, so what can you get ready?

Together, the father and the child co-constructed a plan for the beach that might have been incomplete if the child had done it on his own.

Planning is the process of thinking about and organizing the activities required to achieve a desired goal. It is the forethought (or careful consideration of what will be the necessary steps to complete a future task). Planning takes many forms; therefore, many methods exist to teach your child how to plan. For instance, when throwing a baseball, there is a motor plan, when getting ready there is a timing plan, when dealing with boredom there is a brainstorming plan, and of course when performing a task there is an action plan. Since planning takes place in so many ways, ample opportunities exist to teach planning.

Teach planning.

Motor Plan

A child can learn to throw a ball by placing the ball in his dominant hand. Then, he can put the opposite foot forward. Next, he can hold the arm with the ball behind the head with the arm bent 90 degrees at the elbow. Finally, he can bring the ball hand forward quickly and release the ball as the arm extends in front of the body.

Timing Plan

When getting ready for an event, there is a timing plan. Knowing the movie starts at 2:00 pm and it takes 15 minutes to walk to the theater, we will need to leave between 1:40 pm and 1:45 pm. Before we leave, we will need to eat a quick snack, grab our jackets, and get money in order to pay for the movie. Getting all of these tasks done is going to take about 20 minutes. So we should plan to start getting ready by 1:20.

Brainstorming Plan

When brainstorming, a child asks herself, "What are all of the possibilities?" Sometimes it can help the brainstorming process to ask prompting questions. When dealing with boredom, the child could ask, "What are things I can do in my room?" "What are things that I can do in the garage?" or "What are the things I can do with a friend?" These questions help to generate a bigger list of options that the child can use to conquer boredom.

Delaying Gratification

Learning to delay gratification goes hand in hand with planning. To wait, a child must think ahead about the benefit of being patient. Remember the classic experiment with a child left in a room with a marshmallow? The researcher instructs the child that if he or she does not eat the marshmallow now, he or she will receive 2 marshmallows later. This study demonstrated that at age 4 or 5 years, children start to show the capacity to inhibit the impulse to grab the marshmallow now and the reasoning skills to recognize that 2 treats later would be even better.[29] Parents should teach their child to be patient and that, as in the marshmallow experiment, the rewards for waiting are greater than those for seeking immediate gratification.

Young children are prone to interrupting. "Mom, Mom, Mom" is the mantra of so many preschoolers who demand their mother's immediate attention. Your child may storm into the room when you are cooking, or when you are in the middle of a conversation, or when you are typing on the computer, and say, "Mom, Mom, Mom, I want to buy a new Groovy Girls doll." When this occurs, you have a choice. Stop what you are doing and respond, or use what I call the "wait a minute" technique. Give a stern look, hold up your pointer finger (to indicate "1 minute"), and then wait until you get to a relatively quick, but good, stopping point. Then smile at and thank your child for waiting and answer the question. The training that takes place is the negative reinforcement of a firm look that comes with interrupting and the positive reinforcement of the thank-you and smile that comes with waiting. The goal is to teach your child to politely say, "Excuse me, Mom," and then wait for your attention before asking, "can we go to the park later?" More-detailed strategies are discussed for a school-aged child in the next chapter, Chapter 6, Raising an Organized School-aged Child. For now, it is important to remember that a child's ability to delay gratification shows that forward thinking is occurring.

Anticipating

Anticipating is a form of thinking ahead. Once a child can anticipate an outcome, she is more prepared to make a plan and better able to cope with a disappointing result. Helping your child anticipate a possible change in events can ease the consequences that happen when things don't go as planned. The No. 1 reason why parents bring their children with oppositional behavior to my office is because their children have difficulty tolerating unmet expectations. In other words, when they do not get their way, it stresses them out. This means, for instance, they get upset when their friends want to play something they do not want to play, when they are refused a new toy at a toy store, when their big sister gets to open the hotel door, or when they cannot have more dessert. More often than not, these children share the trait of being unskilled forward thinkers. And thus, they are surprised by seemingly obvious results. They never anticipate, for example, that when playing a game, they may lose, until all of a sudden they are losing and the feeling overwhelms them. The parents of these children tell me that their behavior is better within a routine. In other words, when the child knows exactly what to expect, she behaves best. The routine makes the outcomes more expected; thus, the child does not have to cope with the stress of a "surprising" result. Naturally, then, it is helpful for parents to be consistent and use routines to make the inevitable outcomes more predictable for their children.

A preschool-aged child has budding potential to think ahead, and parents can establish a framework of organization during this period to help develop this skill. A preschool student requires training and practice to develop forward thinking. Be aware that at this age the brain is developing the capacity to plan. Give your preschooler the opportunity to consider options and make plans by encouraging free time, being consistent with schedules and routines so that he can learn to anticipate outcomes, and teaching him to delay gratification.

☑ Recommendations for Forward Thinking in Preschoolers

Practicing Planning

■ Use conversation to co-construct plans and help your child with forward thinking. The way in which you speak to your child and inquire about her thoughts provides the scaffolding for her to consider future events. The words we use, such as *tomorrow*, *next*, and *later*, introduce forward thinking to your child.

■ Be transparent about the plans that you make, and share proposed itineraries to model planning for your child.

■ Break tasks down into steps. Create mini routines and use visual schedules to demonstrate a plan.

■ Let your child narrate picture-only storybooks (eg, *The Snowman*, books by David Wiesner, *Rain and Circus* by Peter Spier), which will challenge your child to consider the author's intent.

■ Show a picture that illustrates the end of a story, and encourage your child to create a short story that tells what led up to this ending.

■ Parents can promote anticipation by previewing situations with their child. Before going to the grocery store, the parent says to the child, "I want you to keep your hands on the cart, and if you can do that in the first 5 aisles, you can pick out a treat." By showing your child what to expect, he can practice thinking ahead. As your children get older, you can help them practice forward thinking by asking them what may be the expected behavior in a situation or the predicted outcome of an event.

Telling Time

■ Introduce your child to a sense of time by using temporal instructions (eg, 1 hour, tomorrow, 1 week). For younger children, associating a time with something they understand (eg, one television show, dinner, bedtime) may help them grasp time concepts.

Delaying Gratification

■ Teach your child to delay gratification by using the "wait a minute" technique.

Transitioning

■ For children with transitional organizational problems, the parents may need to talk explicitly to them about transitions (eg, "Let's have a speedy transition this morning" or "Now, let's slow down during this transition and figure out exactly what we need to take with us"). There can be rewards for days on which the child displays organized transitional behaviors.

Step 5: Promote problem-solving

It is during the preschool years when parents can really begin to see the problem-solving potential of their child. A child at this age demonstrates rapidly increasing independent thought. The hallmark of this age is the statement "I can do it myself." This is great, because the overconfidence that most preschool students possess allows them to get into predicaments, and this challenges them to find solutions. However, your child may not find the best solution or may be unsuccessful. When this happens, find a way to encourage your child's effort. Over the years, your child will have many opportunities to figure things out, so be patient and do not worry about missteps along the way.

My daughter Alexis, the youngest of 5 kids, was brought along to countless rehearsals and athletic practices. These events would have been boring to her, but she always found ways to occupy herself. Sometimes she would befriend another tag-along sibling. She would bring along a toy to play or books to read (with a reminder from her mother). Sometimes she would get lucky when a soccer field was near a playground and we would let her venture over. Keeping an eye on our adventurous 5-year-old made it difficult to watch the soccer game, but such are the sacrifices we parents make. Alexis learned to overcome boredom, which is an important problem-solving exercise for children.

Exploration

Let your child try things and struggle, because learning occurs as we overcome adversity. Instead of providing the solutions for your child, give hints. For example, if your child cannot reach something, perhaps you could suggest that standing on something such as a step stool would make him taller. Don't just get it for him. Let your child earn his success, resulting in increased confidence, which you can reinforce with a timely compliment.

On the other hand, if your child has a timid temperament and she is not inclined to trying things or "putting herself out there," she is at risk for missing out on this period of exploration and the accompanying confidence boost. Safeguard your child from stagnation (task avoidance) by providing encouragement. A timely placed "You can do it!" and then "Nice job!" is critical for a slow-to-warm-up child. Introduce your child to activities slowly to build up her confidence. This may not be the 5-year-old to place onto a soccer team. Instead, take your daughter to the park and kick the ball around with her. Be careful; it may be very easy, and usually quicker, to do things for this child, but, in reality, it is even more important that she learns to do things for herself. The confidence that you show in your child's seemingly fragile ability to solve problems for herself will pay great dividends later.

As your child explores limits and boundaries, she will get herself into difficult predicaments. Knickknacks will get broken, drinks will get spilled, and messes will be made. When this happens, your child may create a story (often bending the truth) to explain the situation. The reality behind the story will usually be transparent, because your child's planning skills are still limited. At this age, children are cognitively at the stage when if asked,

"Did you do this?" they may think, "Hmm, if they are asking me, I have a 50-50 chance they don't know that I did it." So inevitably, they may deny the action. As a parent, you may feel as if your child is lying to you, and technically she is, but do not be phased by the untruthfulness. Your child's explanations are a sign that she is problem-solving. She is trying to give a response that will work best for everyone, without understanding the long-term consequences of telling a falsehood. Address the issue and not the "lie." For instance, if she says she doesn't know how the plant got knocked over, you could say, "When a plant is knocked over, we need to clean it up. Go get the dustpan and we can clean up the mess together." By doing this, you are helping solve the real problem, that is, the spilled plant. Had you reprimanded her for lying, you might have discouraged her future adventures and made her less likely to come to you when accidents happen.

Imagination

Not everything a preschool child does is mischievous. During this phase, creativity blossoms and play skills evolve. As a toddler, your child dabbled in imitative play and functional play (using a toy for its intended purpose). During the preschool years, your preschooler's play skills will evolve from functional play to representational play (using an object to represent another object) and role play (taking on characters). Imaginative play is instrumental to building problem-solving skills. Your child will love to dress up, act out scenes, build, and create. Your 3-year-old may even have an imaginary friend. He may involve his imaginary friend in daily activities, for example, waiting for his friend to finish brushing his teeth before going to bed. Indulge this silliness, because pretend play is practice for the social and emotional roles of life. When your child pretends, he is consciously experimenting with roles and practicing perspective taking. When your child takes on different characters, he has the experience of imagining what it would be like to be them, which can introduce the important developmental skill of empathy. Your role as a parent is to help your child expand on his imaginative journeys. Encourage creative play by providing props and costumes and all the non-battery toys, such as blocks, Lego bricks, dolls, and kitchen sets, that we used when we were kids. Help your child extend his play. Don't let him be content with just being a policeman, but suggest catching a robber or pretending to chase someone that drove through a red light. Don't let him settle for baking pretend cupcakes, but include picking out flavors, picking out icing, and serving the treats. Pretend play is empowering for a child who discovers that he can be whatever he wants by pretending.

If you eavesdrop as your child participates in imaginary play with his toys or friends, you will probably hear some words and expressions you never thought he knew! Pretend play helps your child experiment with different uses of language and methods of expression. In addition, by pretend playing with others, he learns that words give him the means to organize play. This practice will help your child learn to use language to organize his thoughts.

Scripting is not the same as creativity.

Children who tend to repeat the same scripted pretend activities often need more practice in creativity. Scripting is acting out something that a child has seen or memorized. Some children with autism, for instance, are attracted to the character Thomas the Tank Engine. If you give the child either the Thomas train car or the Percy train car, the child may look as if he is pretending, but what he may really be doing is acting out the show he watched last week. Scripting does not exercise simultaneous processing to the same degree as creativity and generalization. Parents can encourage creativity and generalization by providing more-universal toys such as generic cars and dolls, construction sets, and tea sets. These toys are not as easily used to act out a familiar script.

Perspective Taking

Between the ages 4 years and 5 years, cooperative play should develop in your child. Playdates and group activities should be encouraged. Through cooperative play, your child learns how to take turns, share, and creatively problem-solve. Cooperative play has so many complicated elements, but sharing may be the most difficult to learn because this skill requires perspective taking. To learn that the playdate goes better if a playmate is happy takes practice. Beginners may need scaffolding to make these preschooler collaborations successful. A parent can suggest activities (eg, art projects, building, or dressing up) that involve sharing but have enough structure that the playmates know what to do. More-experienced players can operate independently, creating their own activities and reflecting upon the interest of their peers. All that a parent needs to do for experienced playmates is to provide periodic encouragement (eg, "You two are doing such a nice job sharing" or "I love it how you two play together") and reminders to clean up before moving on to the next step.

Summarizing

Summarizing is a good way for you to see whether your child is starting to think about the order of events. A 5-year-old should be able to retell a simple story such as *Goldilocks and the Three Bears*. He should also be able to relay the events of his day. Give your child the opportunity to practice storytelling. Challenge him to share his school day's adventures with you. With practice, he will learn to become more succinct, that is, telling the most important occurrences. Soon he will need to be able to summarize.

Problem-solving With Words

Preschool-aged children can be very funny. One way your child will explore his use of language and understanding of perspective is through comedy. Being funny requires an understanding of what the audience appreciates. At first, your junior comedian may struggle. "Knock, knock." "Who's there?" "Wall." "Wall who?" "There is a wall over there." He tries to imitate the structure of a joke without getting the content. I find that a little bit of sarcasm is a good way to introduce humor. A child needs to understand the big picture to appreciate sarcasm. For instance, if my 5-year-old asks whether he can have dessert before dinner, I might respond with a smile. "Of course you can have dessert. Let's go to the candy store and by all the candy and never eat healthy food again. The dentist will love us." My young detective can tell from the smile on my face and the silliness in my response that I am joking.

Four-year-olds have vocabularies of at least 1,000 words, and most know closer to 5,000 words. By this age, they understand language concepts such as why and where, and now they have sufficient language to understand explanations. Your preschool student is going to ask why a lot. Give clear and concise explanations. Do not just say, "Because I said so," because to do that would be modeling your inflexibility. Your answers are helping your child understand the big picture. Your child might ask, "Why do I have to go to bed, Mommy?" and you can say, "Because little boys that get a good sleep are strong and healthy." With your help, your child has learned a little more about the importance of sleep. If your child is in the habit of responding to all your answers with another question, "Why do boys who sleep get stronger?" then you can encourage your child to do some of the thinking for himself, "Why do you think sleep might be good for a little boy's brain and body?" By doing this, you have given a hint (to the brain) and your child has the opportunity to practice problem-solving.

With the emergence of language comes the ability to reason. Experiments such as the classic marshmallow study, described in the Delaying Gratification section earlier in this chapter, show that around the age of 4 or 5 years, children are beginning to reason. You can support the emergence of this skill by concisely explaining your reasoning. Statements such as "We cannot go out to lunch today because I have to pick up your sister from school and I don't want to be late" or "We won't have time to watch a television show now, because we are leaving to go to the dentist, but when we come home, there will be time to watch something before dinner" model for your child how you reason through problems.

By now, you should realize that opportunities to teach problem-solving are everywhere. How a child plays, explores, and communicates are all practice fields for mental maturation. Going forward, teaching your child to solve problems is one of the most important things you can do to prepare him to be an independent person, who at age 18 will be ready to launch into the world.

Prepare your child for change.

When I'm watching television with our family and my daughter suddenly changes the channel, it drives me bonkers. But if she asks me if she can watch something else in a couple of minutes, it is no big deal, because I have a chance to prepare for a channel change. The analogy of a mental channel changer has been used to refer to a child's ability to shift from one plan to the next. It can be extremely disappointing for a child who has inflexible behavior, for instance, who wants to play hide-and-seek when his friend comes over for a playdate only to discover that the friend wants to play something else. The friend, who has a different plan, is changing your child's mental channel and the stress of not controlling his own channel changer can be overwhelming, resulting in a meltdown. We can support inflexible children by preparing them for change by using schedules, routines, and previewing strategies. These tools are like guides that allow a child to change his own mental channel.

☑ Teaching Problem-solving to Preschool-Aged Students

Imagination

- Provide your child with toys and props that encourage creative pretend play. Baby dolls, action figures, kitchen equipment, construction activities, building materials, and costumes inspire creativity. Your young pretender may like to pretend he is you, so providing him with things from your daily life, such as telephones, grocery bags, or briefcases, could be enough to spark his imagination.

- More-experienced pretenders need less scaffolding and can incorporate objects into their pretend play. Provide access to large cardboard boxes, fabrics, pretend money, and art materials.

- Extend your child's imaginative play by expanding thoughts. "Don't just be a fireman; be a fireman on an adventure." "Don't just bake a cake; celebrate a birthday party." Encourage these activities by playing with your child and extend the fun to new, unique imaginary situations.

- Together with your child, create imaginative stories. Take turns inventing characters, circumstances, and plotlines—this is a great activity for while you're riding together in a car or other modes of transportation.

- Do not worry about your child having imaginary friends. Support the creativity, but do it with a smile on your face so that your child knows that you know the friend is not real.

Perspective Taking

- Provide opportunities for collaborative play. At first, playdates may need some structure (eg, an art project or dressing up) so that the children can work together. Remind the child about sharing and turn taking and the importance of having both friends enjoy themselves.

- Discuss the perspectives of others. One opportunity is when a baby is crying; ask your child why the baby might be upset. Preschool-aged children can be encouraged to think about what a friend might like to play.

Big Picture Thinking

- Encourage the development of your child's sense of humor by being silly, politely sarcastic, and ironic.

Summarizing

- Encourage your older preschooler to summarize. Be patient and listen to his explanations. Ask questions when your child's explanation loses its logic or has gaps. Then repeat back his thoughts using more concise language.

Chapter 6

Raising an Organized School-aged Child: The Master of Routines

The school-age years (ages 5–12) covers a large span during which your children grow in every possible direction. During this time, they are learning manners, rules, and group behavior, as well as solidifying their recognition of, and capacity to follow, routines. When school-aged kids develop interests, they can develop remarkable expertise. They begin to participate in sports, and those who can think strategically about their play can have big advantages. During the school-age period, your child will build friendships and often have a best friend. And, of course, school-aged children go to school where they learn to read and write, and by the end of this period, many are learning algebra. However, there are many organizational challenges that are important for the acquisition of these skills. And if your children's organizational abilities do not progress at the same rate as their learning skills, then, what I have seen happen is, parents fill the void. They wake their kids up for school, manage their homework, prepare their meals, schedule their activities, and clean up after them. Instead of using the school-age years to teach their child to be organized, some parents concentrate on the sport or academic milestones. And when these kids enter high school, unprepared for the organizational challenges, the consequences will become more significant.

From the moment Casey, an 8-year-old, third-grade student, wakes up in the morning, she is a whirlwind of activity. She arrives in the kitchen wearing her pajamas, and her mother promptly reminds her that they will be leaving for school in 30 minutes. Her mother sends Casey back to her room to comb her hair, brush her teeth, and put on her clothes, which her mother laid out last night while putting Casey to bed. Ten minutes later, Casey's mother, who has made breakfast and is waiting for Casey's return, calls for Casey. Casey yells back, "Coming!" and shows up in the kitchen, still wearing her pajamas. "What have you been doing all this time?" asks her mother with a slight tone of annoyance in her voice. "Playing with my dolls," she sulks and then volunteers, "I did brush my teeth." Casey's mom sends her back to comb her hair and get dressed and does not entirely trust that any of her teeth were brushed. Casey returns 10 minutes later. Her mother is already packing up her toast and eggs for her to eat during the ride to school. "How come your socks don't match each other?" "I could not find my other sock?" Casey replies. Her mother starts to explain that they were both there last night but is distracted when she sees Casey turning on the television set. "You've got to be kidding me," scolds her mother. "Your shoes aren't on, you haven't eaten breakfast, and your lunch is not made." Casey puts on her shoes while her mother makes the lunch. The lunch gets made, but the shoes aren't tied, so shoe tying and breakfast eating are relegated for the ride to school. No sooner than they get into the car, Casey declares that she forgot her backpack and races back inside. They arrive to school 5 minutes late, earning Casey her seventh tardy of the year.

When Casey's mother returns home, she is frustrated and exhausted, and when the phone rings, she cringes, because she has a feeling she knows who will be calling. "Mom," says Casey, "I left my homework on my bed."

After an abbreviated expression of exasperation, she goes to find the missing assignment. As she enters Casey's room, she is overwhelmed by the mess. "How can that be," she thinks to herself, "I cleaned this up last night." She starts to clean the room, and underneath the toys she finds the homework and underneath the homework is the missing sock. Feeling embarrassed, she brings the homework to school and hands it to Casey's teacher, not taking the risk of it getting lost again by handing it to Casey.

Organizational teachable moments happen every day in the life of a school-aged child. As a parent, you need to look for these clues and help your child see things differently. The story about Casey shows that simply getting up in the morning and leaving the house presents a multitude of organizational challenges for her. So, as a parent you need to stop and think about the 5 Steps to Raising an Organized Child and help prepare your child for life, not just for school.

Step 1: Be consistent

A school-aged child's growing ability to be persistent and her emerging use of logic can make it even more difficult for parents to respond consistently to their child. School-aged students can get very good at manipulating their parents by either outsmarting them or wearing them down. Your child will point out, for instance, that there are many logical reasons why she should stay up past her bedtime (eg, homework, a special television show, an out-of-town guest, not yet finished with a video game, want to spend more time with Mom and Dad). Yet, each time parents waver, and do not stay consistent on established rules such as bedtime, they damage their credibility. And like an elephant, the school-aged child never ever forgets. She will remember the last time you made an exception and remind you of it, time and time again, to try to work toward what she wants (eg, "But you let me play video games after school last week").

Parents of school-aged children need to be careful to avoid getting caught up in any schemes and arguments of their school-aged child. The way to do this is to always consider the *big picture*. The big picture is the rule that applies or the lesson that the parent is trying to enforce or teach. For instance, in the case of a bedtime, the big picture is that children need 8½ to 11 hours of sleep per night in order to grow and be healthy. Because each breach of the rule will make future enforcement more difficult, only the most important circumstances should be considered. It becomes easier to avoid future arguments when the big picture is **consistently reinforced.** When school-aged children get an answer that they do not want, they will often ask again and again. Parents should not engage in this debate but, instead, should refer to the big picture, "Children your age need sleep to be healthy." If your child has nobody to argue with, he quickly learns that arguing does not work.

At this age, your child will likely make unsafe choices when unsupervised. Therefore, parents need to continue close supervision and limit setting. A school-aged child wants to do many things that he is not old and mature enough to handle, and it is up to parents to establish clear boundaries. Staying up late is just one of them, but there are many, including watching sexually explicit movies, playing violent video games, eating junk food, and riding in the front seat of the car when he is too small, to name just a few. When you say no to allowing your child to participate in these activities that target a mature audience, what you are really saying is "No, because I care about you."

Parents can gradually introduce their children to more freedom and responsibility by allowing them to pursue their interests. A school-aged child will have many things on her plate, such as soccer practices, clubs at school, homework, friends, chores, and family obligations, that will pull the child in many directions, making it even more difficult for her to manage her obligations. As the child enters middle and high school, parents should allow more freedoms, but only as the child proves that she can consistently handle her responsibilities.

Manners should be reinforced during this stage of development. Manners that were used before this age were often parroted. The parent says, "Say, 'Thank you,' Johnny," and Johnny responds, "Thank you." However, at this age, manners should be more automatic. Yet, depending on the circumstance, parents should not expect perfection. When manners are consistently reinforced, a little nod or direct eye contact from a parent ought to be enough to remind the school-aged student to thank someone, clear his plate, or lower his voice in the house. Take care not embarrass your child by reprimanding him in front of others.

Your child will likely have more difficulty regulating his behavior when his physical needs are not met. And yet, kids are not always good about getting enough sleep or feeding themselves on time. When your child is sick, hungry, or tired, he may have more difficulty controlling himself. The best solution is to nip these needs in the bud by making sure your meals are at a certain time during the school week and that bedtime is the same time every night. Be consistent around these important routines. However, during the school-age period, consistency is not always possible, such as after a sleepover. In those instances in which rules need to be bent, we can set consistent expectations. For example, "If you go to a sleepover and stay up late, then remember that you are responsible for your behavior the next day. If you feel cranky, go to your room and get some rest."

A school-aged child is old enough to understand the natural consequences of his actions if natural consequences are consistently reinforced. In the example of a child who behaves poorly after staying up too late at a sleepover, the natural consequence may be that they cannot have sleepovers for another month (until they get older) because they are showing that they are not ready to responsibly handle a sleepover. Another common example occurs when a child cannot turn off a video game. Part of being able to handle the responsibility of screen time (eg, computer and video games, smartphone or iPad games) is knowing when to stop, just like part of an adult being able to drink responsibly is knowing when to stop. If the expectations are clearly explained and your child is unable to unplug after the allotted time has expired, he is not mature enough to use electronics unsupervised. Natural consequences are critical to enforce and prepare your child for life in the real world. The beauty of a natural consequence is that the parent is not the bad guy. As long as the parent has set the expectation in advance, when the child struggles he has only himself to take responsibility. Your child could have fallen asleep earlier at the sleepover, but he chose to stay up past midnight. Really skilled parents can even position themselves on the side of the child (eg, "Oh, that is too bad, because I really like when Johnny sleeps over. I guess when you get a little older, we can do that more often").

The role of the parents of a school-aged child evolves during this time. The parents serve as a coach of the early elementary child, but by the time the child is in middle school, they should step back and be more of a manager. A coach offers suggestions and strategies on how to perform new tasks and provides feedback about day-to-day efforts. The manager is available whenever needed and watches the direction that the child is headed, commenting about trends in the right or wrong direction.

☑ Consistency Recommendations for School-aged Children

- Habits learned during childhood are often carried all the way into adulthood, so consistently sending the message about good habits such as doing chores, regular school attendance, and doing homework is important.

- Remember that it is still the parent's obligation to keep her children safe, so it is important to set limits around safety including no exposure to violent or graphic content, using a car booster seat, wearing a seat belt, and not sitting in the front seat of a car.

- Parents also need to teach their school-aged child healthy habits. Parents should consistently enforce bedtimes, brushing teeth, making healthy food choices, and getting daily exercise.

- As children become more sophisticated and perhaps manipulative in the way they go about pushing limits, parents need to stay on message and focus on the big picture. This will help them be consistent when enforcing rules and limits.

- Consistent enforcement of rules such as cleaning up after making a mess, or giving a toy a time-out when the child uses the toy inappropriately, become increasingly important for school-aged children.

- Avoid making exceptions to rules out of convenience or just to be nice. These exceptions may come back to haunt you when your school-aged child later asks for more.

- Do not get angry when children forget to use manners, but consistently remind them, in a nonconfrontational or non-embarrassing way, to be polite.

- Continue to consistently provide natural consequences instead of punishments for mistakes.

- Parents should be consistent with emotional responses to problems, as this will help children learn to modulate their emotional responses.

Step 2: Introduce order

A metamorphosis of organizational skills takes place in most children during the elementary school years. They enter this period like tiny molecules demonstrating entropy as they move in seemingly random order, bouncing off the walls and into each other, and by the time they exit elementary school, their actions are deliberate, efficient, and mostly independent. Children put order to their universe and begin to recognize that life is full of mini routines that they can master. By early elementary school, they have learned routines of physiology such as toileting, getting dressed in the morning, eating, bedtime, and sleeping. Many 6- and 7-year-olds can do these tasks with a simple prompt and gentle nudging from a parent (eg, "Go get ready for bed" or "It looks like you need to use the bathroom"). By the third grade, with gentle prompting, many can be active participants in managing their daily routines (eg, take a bath or make a lunch). By the end of fifth grade, most students are capable of independence with homework and can prepare for routines such as a practice, a lesson, or a rehearsal. The ability to learn complex routines demonstrates the growth in a child's sequential memory. Younger school-aged children can remember 3 steps, and by middle school, it is reasonable to expect them to remember 4- or 5-step instructions. (See Box 6-1.)

Box 6-1

Routines Performed by School-aged Children With Reminders and Gentle Oversight From a Parent

Five- to 7-Year-Olds

- Getting ready for bed (pajamas and teeth brushing)
- Using the bathroom (wiping, flushing, and washing hands)
- Dressing (picking out clothes and getting dressed)
- Preparing breakfast (getting bowl and spoon, pouring cereal and milk, and eating)

Eight- to 9-Year-Olds

- Taking a bath (plugging tub, pouring water, bathing, and drying off) or a shower
- Preparing lunch (making sandwich, putting into container, and packing sack)
- Following homework instructions (reading directions, executing task, and placing completed work into backpack)

Ten- to 12-Year-Olds

- Gathering and packing items needed for a practice or rehearsal

■ Performing independently with homework (tracking long- and short-term assignments, completing homework, and remembering to turn in completed work)

ADHD can manifest as disorganization.

Attention deficits can sometimes interfere with task follow-through, because distraction prevents registration into memory. If you suspect that attention is a concern, seek medical advice.

Implementing Routines

When your child enters school, you finally have some help in teaching order to your child, because sequences are inherent in the school day. A good teacher will establish daily routines (eg, reading first, spelling time second, recess, and then circle time). There will be rituals for arriving, hanging up jackets, and putting away school lunches. If your child is fortunate, the teacher will be highly organized and consistent with routines. A teacher will teach the steps to projects and support your child's concept of time. School is also one of the first times at which your child's deficiencies may stand out when held up to the standard of his peers. A child who is delayed in sequential awareness (the ability to recognize the order inherent to every task) may struggle at first when he enters school; usually, a talented teacher can get most sequentially delayed children caught up by establishing a clear and consistent structure, but not always. Children who struggle with this function of organization may not pick up on the routines, and sometimes this can be frustrating for the child. Frustrated children often act out, so if your child is misbehaving around times of transition, consider organizational deficiencies as a possible underlying cause.

Things to Consider When a Child Has Problems Following Directions

Five-year-olds can recite the alphabet, by memory. A phone number is 7 digits for a reason: 7 digits is the average recall length for an adult. However, by grouping a number into chunks (eg, 415/555-1212), even a 5-year-old can remember her parent's phone number. When children struggle to remember order, there is often a neurodevelopmental breakdown (a weakness in the brain's thinking abilities). If this is something you notice with your child, call your pediatrician and discuss your observations.

A breakdown in a neurodevelopmental ability is often responsible for a child's struggles to follow directions. Box 6-2 lists the cognitive abilities (or thinking skills) that are important for listening. Children with attention issues, for instance, often demonstrate 2 of these deficits: superficial processing and distractibility. A good example of superficial processing is when one tries to talk to a child while he is watching television. The child appears to be listening and he may even respond with an affirmative exclamation, such as "Mhm." Yet, the child is not thinking about what is being said. The probability that the child remembers to put away his shoes after the show is over is zero. You can ensure your message is delivered by turning off the television set or standing directly in front of your child. Then, ask your child to repeat what you said back out loud. By asking to repeat the message back, a parent can get a pretty good reassurance, whether the message was registered by the child or not.

The other common deterrent to following instructions in children with attention issues is distractibility. One mother told me that "Susie has every intention of helping me out in the morning, but as soon as she leaves my sight to do a simple task, such as getting dressed, she disappears into a world of fantasy. I am always amused by where I will find her and what she will be doing. Of course, when we are running late, it is not always that amusing." Distractions can be internal (eg, a person's thoughts, fears, or fantasies) or external (eg, toys, pets, television). Eliminating as many potential distractions as possible is often necessary to avoid distraction. Over-rehearsing routines can also sometimes reduce internal distractibility. If your child's attention, or continual lack thereof, becomes a cause for concern, seek medical advice from your pediatrician.

The third explanation for problems following direction is a breakdown in sequential memory, which prohibits children from remembering more than 1 or 2 steps at a time. An intact sequential memory opens the door to many academic opportunities. Traditional teaching assumes that students have the ability to remember lectures, spell long words, and remember lists. The brain is a remarkably complex organ, and while concerns about attention and distractibility can influence organization, this chapter focuses on the third concern, that is, breakdowns in sequential memory, because sequential memory is a key component to organization.

Three other explanations for difficulty listening to directions occur infrequently, but they are worth mentioning and often warrant professional help. Some children with language delays may have trouble understanding the direction. If understanding is a concern, misunderstanding should be a consistent problem, as opposed to superficial processing, during which instructions are inconsistently followed. If your child consistently misunderstands information, consult with your pediatrician and seek a language evaluation. Other children can be inflexible and so reflexively say no to everything. These children do not follow instructions. There are reasons why children who lack organization can be oppositional, which is discussed later in this chapter in the Step 4: Practice forward thinking section. For these children, consultation with a psychologist or developmental pediatrician can be helpful. Finally, sometimes, missing instructions leads to a diagnosis of a hearing loss. Talk with your pediatrician about seeking help from an audiologist if this is a concern.

Box 6-2

Common Explanations for Why a Child Does Not Follow Directions

- Superficial processing
- Distractibility
- Insufficient sequential memory
- Poor comprehension
- Positive gain or unintentional reward for negative behavior, anxiety, or depression
- Hearing deficits

Teaching Order

Just like a plant needs to be watered, a student must be challenged to grow. Parents and teachers should constantly coach students to master their organizational skills by challenging them to perform managerial tasks. The key is not to push a child to do what is expected at a certain age; instead, successful parents encourage their children to do slightly more than they can do today, and tomorrow, and the next day. As with any learning task, coaching can be time intensive at first, but it gets easier over time. Often it would be convenient for parents to manage their child's organizational tasks themselves, but this practice hinders a child's learning and leads to later frustrations for parents and children. Overly doting parents tend to raise dependent children.

As always, consistency is an important theme for teaching concepts, and sequences and routines are no exception. Continue using the routines of early childhood for activities such as bedtimes and mealtimes. Introduce new routines for self-help (eg, preparing their own sport bag with a new water bottle and their cleats for practice, packing a healthy lunch for school) and responsibilities (eg, homework and chores). Remember that as each new routine is introduced, at first your child will most likely need a great deal of scaffolding in order to be successful. Set your child up to be successful by gradually pushing toward independence. It is unrealistic to suddenly tell your child that from now on he will need to responsible for feeding the dog every morning before school and expect perfection. Fido is going to be hungry if that task is not supervised. At first, you may need to remind him each morning and then, over time, transition to posting a reminder. If he does forget, have a conversation about what strategies he needs to implement to be more successful.

A school-aged child's tendency is to develop his self-competence, and he demonstrates this by asserting independence and resisting external controls. The tendency to push boundaries and resist limitations is developmentally appropriate, but it is also part of what makes parenting difficult. We want our children to question things that do not make sense and seem dangerous or unfair, but we also want them to understand that certain routines need to happen for a home to function. Do not be detoured by emotional outbursts; children occasionally need to let off steam because they have not mastered emotional regulation (the ability to control mood and behavior in a given situation). I wish I could give you a strategy that will make parenting easy, but consistent routines and boundaries will at least make teaching your child easier. Consistency tells your child that certain rules are not negotiable, because you are conveying the point that "This is how our family operates." If you can be consistent, your child will learn that it is not worth protesting some things. A parent's job never ends; daily consistency is critical, because, when children are left to their own limitations, routines can quickly break down and the behavior of children can become difficult to manage. Also, when parents are consistent, they model this behavior for their children. An effective parent of a school-aged child offers the opportunity for independence but provides daily oversight and reminders (when needed) about expectations.

The themes of starting and completing projects and time management become a major focus for teaching sequential organization to a school-aged child. When children were younger, we taught them that every task had a beginning, a middle, and an end primarily by having them clean up after themselves. The school-aged child can apply his organizational skills to projects and homework (Box 6-3). As an example, writing a book report can illustrate the many steps that are integrated into daily school projects. A good student will read the assignment instructions before starting a project; then read the book (while possibly taking notes), plan out what to discuss by making an outline, write the assignment, and edit the finished project; and then remember to turn the work in on time. A major goal for a school-aged student is to learn how to identify all the steps that are inherent in a project. Until children acquire these skills, parents need to coach their children on how to approach their homework. When guiding your student, remember that it is even more important to teach the organizational process than to perfect the homework assignment.

Box 6-3

Homework Steps

1. Recording the assigned tasks
2. Bringing home necessary materials
3. Performing each piece of homework
4. Putting completed materials into the designated folder in the backpack
5. Turning homework into the teacher on time

Time Management

In a society where our children are overscheduled, there are many opportunities for children to learn about time. Allow your child to participate in the creation and management of his own schedule. It is instinctive for parents to prepare children for transitions and herd them from school, to the soccer field, and to music lessons. However, doing this deprives them the opportunity to think about time for themselves.

I am not suggesting that we need to overschedule our kids. One training technique that parents of uber-scheduled children should consider is to occasionally have their older school-aged child go outside and play but plan to be home by 5:30 for dinner. Now the child is encouraged to think about time on his own. He not only needs to get home on time but must also consider what activities are realistic to start and finish in the amount of time he has been given: this is the beginning of time management.

Starting and Finishing

Getting started and learning to finish a project can be very difficult for many children. Too much time is spent worrying about a project, wondering what to do, or even wondering how to get started. When needed, give your child a jump start. You can do this by offering a suggestion or showing an example of a completed product. One excellent teacher told me that when she assigns essay writing, she likes to write the first and last sentences for some of her disorganized students. She found that the students were generally able to write logically from the beginning to the end when they were given this push and target. Eventually, they learned to write their conclusions on their own. She found that learning to write topic sentences took the longest, perhaps because when beginning a project, there are so many options that it takes a lot of working memory (planning) to figure out where to start.

Throughout the elementary and middle school years, students should be reminded to become "closers." In baseball, the closer makes sure a baseball game ends successfully by pitching in the last inning when a team has a lead. Managers of Major League Baseball teams recognize the significance of closing. Baseball games are not over until the last out is made. Managers have developed a specialized pitcher called a *closer* to finish games. This pitcher is usually one of the team's hardest-throwing and mentally toughest pitchers, and often these pitchers have a bit of an edge to them. "Goose" Gossage, Trevor Hoffman, Lee Smith, and Dan Quisenberry were successful closers because they seemed to forget about their mistakes almost instantly and could focus on one thing: getting the batter standing in front of them out. It is difficult to say where players like this come from, but there is a baseball term used whenever speaking about a closer: "grooming." A team selects a hard-throwing pitcher and grooms him to be the team's closer. Perhaps they put these pitchers through increasingly stressful situations to see how they can maintain focus on their objective, to make the last out. To achieve success, children need to be closers, and schools and parents should start preparing their children from a very young age.

In life, "closing" means making sure tasks are thoroughly performed. In school, this means checking your work, going back and rereading your essay for mistakes, or making sure a report is complete and presented neatly. Unfortunately, for many school children, neatness counts more than we realize. Teachers do not like deciphering a student's work. Closing a written assignment means taking the extra time to write neatly, type, check your spelling, and do whatever it takes to not only complete the work on time but also present it in a readable format. At home, closing entails, for instance, putting away what one takes out or cleaning up after oneself. It is very likely that your child will need many reminders throughout this period of time before he learns to finish what he starts, because many school-aged children do not master this skill until high school. However, by keeping rewards contingent upon completing tasks (eg, "We can leave after the game is all cleaned up" or "You can have dessert after you put away your dinner dish"), parents can help their child learn to close at a younger age. (See Box 6-4 for attributes of good closers.)

Box 6-4

Attributes of Good "Closers"

Good "closers"...

- Remember to flush the toilet.
- Consistently clean up after themselves.
- Turn in completed assignments.
- Finish projects neatly.
- Appropriately end conversations.
- Bring home materials and books needed for homework completion.
- Place their dirty dishes into the dishwasher.
- Do not forget their sweatshirts, jackets, cleats, and other needs on the playground at school or at the gym or field after practice.

Your successful student exits middle school with a sense of independence and self-confidence. He has developed time management skills and can perform a myriad of independent tasks. He manages his homework, he helps with chores around the house, and he will be ready for high school.

✓ Sequencing Recommendations for School-aged Children

Teaching Order

- Schedules should be used to teach the concept of time. Daily itineraries can be displayed on large sheets of paper or on a whiteboard. Parents and teachers should reference the schedule frequently throughout the day.
- Calendars can be used to help keep track of appointments, practices, and deadlines.

- Sequential activities that can help develop skills in your school-aged child are cooking from recipes, playing a musical instrument, and keeping a personal calendar or journal.

- Parents and teachers can lead children into a task by performing the first step of a project. A jump start can take on many forms. A parent can jump-start a project by cleaning up the first few toys, starting the bath, putting toothpaste onto the toothbrush, or writing the first sentence of a paragraph.

- Rehearsal is needed to remember sequences. With younger children, verbal drills can be used to strengthen the rapid recall of practical sequences such as the alphabet, counting series (1s, 2s, 3s, 5s, and 10s), forward and backward (for 2- to 4-year-olds), the days of the week and months of the year (for 4- to 6-year-olds), and multiplication tables (for 7- to 10-year-olds).

- Continue to be consistent with limit setting. Remember that cause and effect is the most basic sequence. Therefore, natural consequences for a student's actions are an important way to emphasize a fundamental of sequential organization.

- Many games promote the development of sequential memory; 2 favorites are Simon and Bop It! (Computer games are not good substitutes because most require very little sequential memory.)

Getting Started and Finished

- By showing an example of a completed project, parents and teachers may actually help students visualize how to get started. It is also helpful for teachers to build "getting started" time into activities, by creating project timelines that include initiating tasks.

- Emphasize completion: Teach your children to turn in finished work and clean up their work space after a project. Parents should always gently remind thoroughness when tasks are left incomplete.

- Parents should make daily use of "closing" terminology and phrases (eg, "When we are finished," "When it is done," "After we complete," "The last thing we need to do").

■ School-aged children should be encouraged to finish conversations with an ending (eg, "I will see you later," "Nice to meet you," "Thank you," "Goodbye").

Implementing Routines

■ Complicated procedures such as writing an essay or long division can be displayed like a recipe in a cookbook. Most of us can't make a chocolate cake on our own, but we can follow a recipe. And, if we bake enough cakes over time, eventually, it will become engrained in our memory. The same goes for schoolwork. Providing "recipe cards" to kids may help them perform and understand the material before they are able to memorize the information.

■ Be sure to hold your child accountable for reasonable routines such as washing hands after using the bathroom, taking off shoes before entering the house, clearing the table after eating, and editing a writing assignment before turning it in.

■ If your child has problems remembering to bring home books and materials needed for homework, encourage him to bring all his materials home by using a daily checklist or keeping a separate set of textbooks at home. An e-mail to the teacher for support on this might be helpful too. More and more students now have online access to textbooks, so be sure to investigate this option as a possible tool when an item or assignment is forgotten.

Time Management

■ Parents and teachers can help develop time management skills with children.
- As students enter middle school, they can be given time deadlines, but manage their time in the interim (eg, "Be home by 5:00 pm" or "Clean up your room by the time Grandma arrives at noon").
- Weekly meetings can be set up to help plan the academic, social, and exercise schedules for the week. The student can then record the daily time spent on each activity. Parents and teachers can review the log and reflect on how time was managed during the week, with suggestions for refining the plan.

■ When first creating the schedules, parents and children should discuss how long each activity is likely to take. Breaks should be included and time for spontaneous, unscheduled events accounted for as well.

Sequential Order Accommodations

■ Pencil control is a sequential finger movement. A child who struggles to write can bypass this by using dictation (using a microphone to talk into a computer). If finger sequencing continues to be an issue in later elementary school, handwriting can be very problematic. Allow older students to type, which is a simpler sequential task, instead of writing. Having your child practice typing on the computer will help as he gets older.

■ Provide your child with lists for ordinary occurrences such as homework, packing, and chores, and then, as he gets older, teach him to make his own lists. Lists can serve 2 important functions: they show the steps in a procedure and they serve as a bridge to independence for a child. When using a list, children no longer need the parent to remind them about each step. Instead, the parent can simply direct them to their list. For younger children who are still learning to read, picture lists are valuable.

■ Systematic strategies for improving long-term retention and retrieval of information are referred to as mnemonic strategies. Acronyms are one commonly used mnemonic device (eg, using the letters H, O, M, E, and S [HOMES] to represent the names of the Great Lakes; Roy G. Biv for the colors of the rainbow). The acronym is a cue that is used when the information is being learned, and recalling the cue when taking a test will help your child remember the information. Other popular mnemonic devices include rhyming (eg, "*i* before *e*, except after *c*," "sounded as *a*, as in *neighbor* or *weigh*") and singing (eg, the traditional alphabet tune, current attempts to use rap music to teach concepts to children who enjoy that type of music).

Step 3: Give everything a place

Location

Many of the placement routines you created for your toddler should still be part of your daily routine. As your child moves through elementary school, you can hold him more accountable to complete visual routines with fewer reminders. Add maintaining his school notebooks, backpack, and activity bags as part of his visual routine. Activity bags are a great way to chunk things together. His soccer bag may include a ball, shin guards, soccer cleats, a protein bar, and a water bottle. After each practice, he can be reminded to stock the bag and put it where it goes so that it is ready for the next practice. Before he leaves for practice, he can take a quick inventory to make sure everything is in the right place. If your child struggles to remember where things go, preventing him from completing any of his spatial expectations (eg, room, backpack, activity bags), try making a list so that he can check daily to make sure things are in place. These lists are visual-sequential representations of the new chunk of information that your child is trying to learn.

Your child's teacher will help teach visual organization too. Like with items in your house, the teacher knows that in the classroom, everything should have a place. Kindergarten teachers insist on the consistent use of systems. For instance, some teachers give each student a folder that is loaded with papers and notes to be brought back and forth to school every day. Encourage your child to follow homework routines by helping him check his homework folder nightly when he is a young student, and in later elementary school, help him perhaps weekly, or even more infrequently. Occasional backpack checks will also be needed.

If your child finds it difficult to organize his materials, simplify the visual information for him. At times when I entered my children's kindergarten classrooms, I was overwhelmed. I wondered how they could possibly learn in that situation. I realize that the job of a kindergarten teacher is equal parts learning and stimulating to spark interest, so visual excitement is important. At home, we can give our child individualized attention and it is therefore easier to stimulate him with interaction, allowing us to scale back on the visual overstimulation. Limit the number of toys that are on display in the house. Put toys that are not currently being used into bins in the back of the closet. Some parents have found that taking the box springs off the frame and dropping it to the floor prevents toys from being lost under the bed. Label items in the room so it is clear to him where everything goes. Simplifying your child's space will make organizing easier for him.

Symptoms of Spatial Disorganization

When the brain misplaces, or cannot retrieve, visual information, affected children appear messy and their rooms are untidy; their clothes, rumpled; and their hair, uncombed. Students seem irresponsible. They misplace their homework, leave their books at school, and leave their jackets on the playground. Parents grow increasingly frustrated as their children do not learn from their past mistakes. Teachers underestimate the capabilities of children whose disorganization prevents them from demonstrating how they can perform. Common issues include

- Misplacing or losing items
- Messy desks, backpacks, and rooms
- Trouble remembering faces and past events
- Weak pattern recognition
- Possible delayed acquisition of spelling and sight-word reading
- Difficulty grasping geometric concepts
- Poor coordination

Organization for a school-aged child means moving a dependent child toward independence. The school-aged child leaves home for extended periods of time and is expected to transport items back and forth between home and school. The student is responsible for making sure that messages come home and homework returns to school on time. Parents need to continually reinforce the use of systems to compensate for emerging spatial organizational skills. Remember, do not expect mastery of cleanup until your kids graduate from college—ability and motivation have to line up before mastery takes place.

The visual system is fully developed for most children by the time they finish elementary school. A school-aged child is capable of not just seeing but organizing and understanding visual information just as well as adults. Although he may be capable of processing this information, it does not necessarily mean that your school-aged child is skilled at using this part of his brain. Parents can continue to provide opportunities for their child to learn how to process visual information. How the brain interprets and uses visual information becomes increasingly important during the school years. Reading, playing ball, going to new places, using and managing a backpack, meeting new people, and cleaning up bigger messes all challenge your school-aged child's visual system.

It is easy for a child to become overwhelmed by all the visual excitement that surrounds him. The first time you walk into a kindergarten classroom, you will understand what I am talking about. A typical kindergarten classroom is plastered with visually stimulating materials everywhere. The walls are each covered with colorful number lines, the alphabet, days of the week, and months of the year, and student artwork hangs from the ceiling. The shelves are filled with books to read and art supplies and other school materials. You can help your school-aged child understand the relative importance of this visual content by simplifying visual systems, "chunking together" visual content, and putting order to the visual information, by giving everything a place.

Spatial Language

Reading is the greatest visual milestone of the school-age years. Reading opens the door to learning, and those children who read well tend to enjoy learning more. Reading depends on visual recognition and rapid naming (skills learned mostly by exposure and practice), but because kids get bored when parents drill with flash cards, parents need to find other ways to make learning fun. Read to your child daily. When my children were young, I would read to them and we would play games such as having them follow along and point out high-frequency words (eg, *it, the, and*). When I would come to one of those words, I would pause and wait for them to chime in. When we finished reading, I would thank them for helping me. When they started reading aloud, I was careful not to correct them, but when they skipped words, I might point at the word they skipped, or when they read something that made the sentence silly, I might laugh with them. Some parents find that labeling objects around the house helps strengthen their child's association between the written word and an object. When we talk about this strategy, I always picture the family dog walking around with a Dog sign taped to its back.

Spatial Games

Visual matching and visual memory games can be used to develop the muscles needed for reading. Many games are designed to encourage children to rapidly make associations, visualize patterns, and match similar objects. Games listed in Box 6-5 challenge some of the same skills needed for reading, so playing games such as these may actually improve your child's chances of being a good reader.

Box 6-5

Games That Develop Visual Memory and Visual Recognition

Memory or Concentration	Perfection
(card game)	Senior Moments
Diggity Dog	Sherlock Holmes
Gotcha!	Shopping List
Guess Who?	Simon
Make 'N' Break	Stare!
Mastermind	Tonga Island
Match 'n' Turn	

During the school-age years, parents should continue to give their student the opportunity to develop her visual processing skills through play. Much of the play of younger students should be building, constructing, and artwork. The more they explore the physical properties of objects, the more they will understand visual-spatial relationships between objects. So give your young school-aged child Lego bricks, Erector sets, Zoob sets, and anything else she may want to build with. Let her explore various art media such as painting, drawing, pottery, origami, and sewing—all these will help her put order to her world. When she gets older, you can show your child how to use more-adventurous building opportunities. With adult supervision, you can show her how to use your hammer, a glue gun, and a drill so that she can build and create. Some computerized building games also exist, such as the universally popular Minecraft. Although research on the benefits of computer games is limited, some likely can also help develop visual processing centers (the part of the brain whose job it is to understand and remember sensory information from the eyes). Parents should consider limiting screen time (eg, computer games, video games, iPad use, and phone use) per day because screens are generally less social, require less imagination, encourage physical stagnation (discourage exercise), and tend to be more addicting than other types of interactive play.

Ball play will help develop the visual tracking and processing skills of your school-aged child. By age 5, children are usually capable of catching and throwing a small ball, making this type of play more fun for your child and for you. There are 2 types of ball play to consider for your child: static and dynamic. Static ball play happens in games during which your child controls the movement. Some examples of static ball play include golf, bowling, shooting basketball free throws, hitting baseballs from a tee, boccie, and billiards. These types of activities may be easier for your child to learn at first but are difficult to perfect because they require precision. In dynamic play, your child needs to react to the movement of the ball. Sports such as tennis, soccer, basketball, catching a baseball, and table tennis are examples. These activities take longer to master, but they can be learned in stages and taught at first while the ball movement is controlled. When attempting to learn a new dynamic visual-motor activity (eg, hitting a baseball), break the task down into its components. Hitting, for example, consists of the swing of the bat, recognizing the location of the ball, and calculating the timing of contact. So, after practicing properly swinging the bat, the player can hit a ball from a baseball tee, or hanging from a string, and then finally attempt hitting a ball pitched to her. Likewise, soccer players begin by practicing trapping, kicking with each foot, and juggling the ball before progressing to scrimmages on the field. Playing ball sports will help your child process spatial information.

Children do not need to be athletes to develop their spatial skills; some data suggest that playing music can develop spatial processing, among other abilities. Psychological and neuroscientific research demonstrates that musical training in children is associated with many important skills ranging from verbal talents to reasoning skills. The theory is that the brain grows important circuits as children practice playing their instruments.

A meta-analysis of 15 separate studies indicated that music instruction enhanced performance on certain spatial tasks that resulted in improved scores on the Object Assembly (a visual-spatial task) subtest of the Wechsler Intelligence Scale for Children.[30] Another study by Costa-Giomi noted that children taking piano lessons improved their visual-spatial skills during the first 2 years of music instruction.[31] So introduce your child to music. When he is young, let him bang on tambourines and form marching bands. Have crazy dance parties. Then, if your child shows any interest, encourage music lessons. Although music and ball sports are not the only ways to develop good visual tracking and spatial skills, research clearly shows that they help.

Spatial Chunking (Grouping)

Right now, you might be wondering what reading, music, and ball sports have to do with the concept of giving everything a place. All these things are related because they all depend on and help develop the visual processing system (the part of the brain responsible for understanding and remembering sensory information from the eye) that is needed to organize your child's world. Remember that an adept visual processor has a great organizational advantage because visual information is, by definition, chunked together. In the Step 2: Introduce order section earlier in this chapter, I explain that an important organizational skill is to create mini routines so that tasks can be remembered as a whole. With visual processing, it is natural to picture and then remember content as a whole. For instance, a child may be able to view in his mind's eye what goes into each of his dresser drawers, or where things hang in his closet, or better yet, where everything goes in his room. Visual chunking also is helpful when reading. This is the concept between whole-word reading and sight-word reading. As soon as a child can transition from sounding out the sequence of words to sight words (word recognition), his reading rate speeds up. It is more efficient to remember visual information as a whole than it would be to remember as a list or sequence. How do you teach visual chunking? By giving everything a place.

Memory plays a critical role in being organized.

On a neurodevelopmental level, the process of being organized is complex and involves the synchronized efforts of multiple brain components, but the memory system and the executive functions (the ability to plan, organize, and complete tasks) work together and take on the greatest role in that process. The executive functions are involved in both the proper filing of information and the efficient retrieval of information from the memory system, which is capable of storing data for a lifetime. The brain's memory is a massive filing system capable of storing many different types of important, and sometimes trivial, bits of information. Children who lack organization either ineffectively sort information into memory or are unable to retrieve memories at will, or both. They have trouble remembering where things need to be, what to do, and when they need to do it. An organized student remembers what homework he has to complete, performs the work, and then remembers to turn it in on time.

 ## Spatial Skill Recommendations for School-aged Children

Giving Everything A Place

- Continue to use zones in the home where certain activities and items are kept—everything still has a place. Students need an established area to do homework, a place for electronics, and a spot for shoes, among other stations.
- Simplify your child's environment. Organize her room, play, and work areas. Put away unused and unneeded toys. Parents can streamline their child's room by labeling items on shelves and drawers. Clear storage bins could

also provide visual cues to remind the child where to store toys, books, and other objects.

- A child should be encouraged to keep his or her possessions in the same place every day.

- Teachers can demonstrate the value of organization by allowing 5 minutes each day, and 10 minutes at the end of each week, for the children to organize their desks, folders, and backpacks.

- Teachers can also develop clear systems for keeping track of completed and uncompleted work. For example, each student could have an individual hanging file in which she can place completed work and the teacher could allow forgetful students to immediately turn in homework assignments upon entering the classroom each morning.

- Students can use color-coded folders and notebooks to help organize assignments for different academic subjects.

- Set up spatial expectations or responsibilities. The expectations can be similar for younger and older students, but younger students require reminders as often as daily. The following expectations are reasonable for school-aged children:

  - After breakfast: Clear plate.
  - After school: Put shoes and backpack away.
  - After homework: Put homework into notebook and notebook into backpack.
  - Sports: Keep sporting equipment in a bag (eg, soccer ball, cleats, and shin guards; baseball glove, bat, ball, and cap).
  - After dinner: Clear plate to sink. Older children can put dishes into dishwasher.
  - After shower: Put dirty clothes into hamper and hang up towel.

Spatial Language

- Have your young child follow and give spatial directions. For instance, "Go to the table and look underneath it to find the missing ball." Older children can improve their spatial awareness by learning and teaching directionality.

- A student could verbally explain how to get from one place to another in school, or draw or create a visual map to illustrate her home, school, or neighborhood.
- An aspiring athlete could diagram plays for a team sport.

Spatial Toys

- Encourage play that promotes spatial awareness, such as art, puzzles, and building. Some games provide excellent spatial exercise, such as the card game Memory or Concentration, or Connect Four, Make 'N' Break, Perfection, Guess Who?, and Jenga.
- Arts and crafts provide excellent opportunities for spatial planning because when painting a picture, for instance, a child generally operates from a mental plan.
- Construction toys (eg, Lego bricks, Lincoln Logs) provide another opportunity for a child to work from a plan. At times, the child can practice following the design on the package insert, but the child should also be encouraged to build his or her own original creations.
- Many musical instruments, such as the piano, the guitar, or drums, promote cognitive development and challenge children to develop their motor-spatial planning skills.
- Ball sports promote spatial awareness because they require the mind to perform mental calculations as the eyes track balls while they roll on the ground or fly through the air.

Spatial Awareness

- Encourage your young school-aged child to write within double lines, and graph paper can be used to help students line up and organize math calculations.
- Teach math using spatial representations to complement numerical equations. For instance, fractions can be demonstrated as wedges of pizza.
- By the time your children enter the third grade, be sure they have a handle on the use of introductory mathematical graphs and tables.

■ Reading is a visually loaded task and can promote the development of visual memory. When a child moves from decoding to word recognition, reading rate improves. This is because the child is now relying on visual memory. Daily reading is important for students in order to keep developing spatial recognition of words and how to spell more-complex vocabulary.

■ Practice handwriting and cursive so that the brain can become more efficient at planning appropriate spacing for letters and words and how to connect each letter to the next.

Step 4: Practice forward thinking

Tremendous growth in forward thinking usually takes place during the school-age years. However, teachers will attest that among students, there is a remarkable range in organizational ability at this age. Some children enter middle school still needing daily hand-holding, while others are organizational experts capable of handling their daily routine and in some cases looking out for others, such as their friends or younger siblings. When my wife was 11 years old, she was babysitting 3 children younger than 5 years. She was preparing their food, changing diapers, and getting them ready for bed—tasks that many parents struggle to perform. It is no wonder we have raised 5 independent children! I am no organizational slouch, but I was a much later bloomer than my wife. When I was 14, I remember my parents asking my 15-year-old neighbor to check in on me when they left me home alone, because they trusted her more than they trusted me. Nobody was leaving their 3 children in my care until I was much older. Given that so much variation exists in the development of forward thinking, parents and teachers should make an effort to understand each child's individual level and encourage the child's acquisition of the next level skills.

The goal of many middle school teachers is to get their students ready to be independent high school students. Some do this by introducing independence at the same rate to all students. Some children are ready for this challenge and thrive in middle school, but some otherwise capable children struggle because of the organizational demands placed upon them. They do not bring home what is needed, and they forget to turn in the work that they complete. They are lost in the expectations that they either missed or forgot during the day. Remember what a tumultuous time middle school was? Every student is trying to fit in. You are now moving from classroom to classroom. Imagine what it would be like for a middle school student struggling to keep up, getting poor grades, and having his parents constantly disappointed. Under these circumstance, it is easy to see why a child might give up. Perhaps the best solution is to acknowledge the differences in organizational skills and allow for supervision as needed. As necessary, parents could be taught to activate different levels of homework supervision with the goal for them to gradually disengage from the process (Box 6-6). In addition, students could be given a grade for organization and a separate score for their academics, which should measure the mastery of a subject and not the ability to turn work in on time.

Box 6-6

Levels of Parent-Teacher Homework Support

1. Teacher-parent oversight: Teacher signs student homework log or uses online scheduling system daily. Parents sign completed homework. This way, it is easy to track where a breakdown might occur (eg, not bringing work home, not completing work, not turning in work).
2. Parent supervision: Parents check daily homework and help student with homework plan.

3. Teacher supervision: Teacher notifies parent immediately if homework is missing.
4. Parent long-term planning: Parents help student with just long-term assignment planning.
5. Relaxed supervision: Teacher notifies parent if child is falling behind.
6. Parent consultant: Student is on his own to succeed or fail, but parents are available when the student asks for help.

Managing Schedules

A school-aged child is often very busy. Choir, soccer, theater, piano, baseball, and all other types of clubs or lessons after school seemingly necessitate an assistant for your child to manage her schedule. Parents often fill the void of the assistant by handling all the details. While involving your student in planning may be more complicated and occasionally result in mistakes, it is important to challenge your student to be involved in managing her schedule. Make sure she thinks about getting prepared for each task in advance. Students can think about time and materials needed for homework, activities, exercise, and play.

Some families do not have the luxury to enroll their children in afterschool activities, leaving their children with hours of free, and often unsupervised, time. In these circumstances, it may be even more important to work with a child to develop an appropriate schedule. You and your children can agree on time spent exercising, doing chores, reading, doing homework, and relaxing. You can discuss healthy after-school snacks and even ask for their help with a dinner plan. We are all more effective when we have a plan or a schedule, and parents can model order no matter the circumstance.

Predicting and Estimating

The young student can learn to make predictions about the future. Academically, *forecasting* is often called *estimating*. First through fourth grade students are actively taught this process. For example, they are encouraged to round up and round down to the nearest tenth or hundredth so that an easier calculation can be made, and this calculation can be compared with the actual (correct) answer. Reinforce for your child the importance of this process, as it provides a great opportunity to think ahead. However, forward thinking is not limited to math. One of my favorite thinking-ahead teaching strategies is to make predictions about what is going to happen in a book. Read with your elementary school student and ask questions such as "What is going to happen next?" "Do you think he will escape?" or "Will the dog find its way home?" These questions prompt your child to listen and think at the same time. In doing so, we are building "simultaneous processing muscles," the force that drives forward thinking.

Predicting can also be done to guide a behavior. Most children are not always skilled with their social choices, but they can understand that behavior is a choice. In my office, I teach this concept by using hindsight to guide forethought. After a child makes a social mistake, I might encourage the parent to ask, "Was that a helpful choice or an unhelpful choice?" Then without passing judgment, I might encourage the parent to have the child make a prediction about the future, such as "What could you do next time?" My intent is to bring to conscious a planning process that is usually subconscious or automatic for most people.

Hindsight to Guide Forethought

One student told me that he "always makes stupid mistakes." Having known that he was a very intelligent boy, I told him that he "is very talented" and asked him what he meant by "stupid mistakes." He said, "The other day, I was hanging out with a group of friends. We were all making fun of our teachers. Then I said, 'My Spanish is not very good, but I am pretty sure I heard the Spanish teacher say that he sleeps with goats.' When nobody laughed, I looked around my circle of friends and saw the Spanish teacher's daughter.

I always make those kinds of mistakes." This student is intelligent and kind, but comments such as this come out too easily. So I asked him what he did after he said that, and he said, "Nothing, I was just so embarrassed that I looked at the ground until other people started talking." Then I asked him what he thought he could do differently next time. He said, "I can try to take more time to think before I speak." Knowing that self-monitoring can be very difficult for an impulsive child, I suggested that he also practice his skills at apologizing and he agreed. Together, we used hindsight to make a plan for the future. Talking through real life examples can help children feel better.

Punishing children for mistakes is generally an ineffective teaching strategy. Parents of children who are very impulsive should remember that their behavior can often be unfiltered. Therefore, if a thought pops into their mind, they just act on it. In this case, they might not have the time to make a choice. In these instances, I suggest to teach them by using hindsight in hopes that they realize that next time, it would be better to think ahead. This technique will reinforce a much needed skill that they can use once their frontal lobe (the part of the brain responsible for organized thinking) begins to mature and they get better at filtering before they act.

An organized student uses estimation when studying for a test. While a disorganized, but dedicated, student prepares by studying all the material, the organized student predicts what is going to be on the test and then focuses his efforts on the topics that are most important, allowing him to master what the disorganized student barely has time to review. Predicting a teacher's testing pattern is a skill that requires practice.

Being Prepared

A child who can think ahead is more likely to be prepared. It is clear how preparation improves performance (academic, athletic, social, or artistic), but the benefits of being prepared are subtler when it comes to the topic of behavior. If your child does not bring a pencil to school, it is very difficult to take notes. If your child does not practice playing the piano in between lessons, it will be very difficult to excel at a recital. Less obvious, however, is how being prepared improves behavior. Consider any transition your child needs to make, such as turning off the computer to come to dinner. If you surprise your son by walking in and turning off the computer, there is nearly a 100% certainty he will react, possibly even explode. Instead, if the rule is that the computer must always be turned off by 6:00 pm for dinner, and you give him reminders at 5:45 pm and 5:55 pm, he is more likely to save his "work" and transition smoothly. Being prepared does not guarantee a successful transition, but it certainly helps.

Being prepared starts with setting a goal—a good place to start when learning a plan. The goal need not be lofty like becoming an astronaut or winning a game. Goals can be as simple as what a child wants to do today. These basic daily goals are critical because they emphasize to your child that every task can have a target result, such as finishing homework by 7:00 pm, getting ready on time, or finishing a chapter in a book. Help your child set realistic goals. For example, winning a basketball game or a season may be unrealistic because too many variables exist (eg, injury, the play of the other team, the officiating), but it is realistic to set a goal of being a 70% free-throw shooter or being able to complete 50 push-ups. Bring goal setting to the forefront of your child's mind by asking about the goals he has set for himself. Once a goal is in place, you can help your child think through how to plan appropriately.

Planning Ahead

The first step in planning is to set a goal. Once a goal is set, you can help your school-aged child with the remainder of a plan. The plan may include gathering materials or practicing a skill so that he is prepared, for instance, for an after-school activity or taking a test. In the previous chapter, Chapter 5, Raising an Organized Preschooler, I demonstrate how to use conversations to co-construct a plan with a preschool-aged child. This same process can be used with a school-aged child who is now likely ready to take a greater role in the planning conversation. Remember, it is the parent's job not to make the plan but to encourage planning with questioning. For instance, here is a sample conversation with an 11 year-old boy.

Mother: You have a baseball game today after school.

Son: What time?

Mother: Right after school, so I am going to pick you up and we will head over to the game.

Son: I better pack my stuff now so you can bring it with you when you pick me up.

Mother: Good idea, and what are you going to pack?

Son: My uniform and glove.

Mother: Anything else?

Son: Oh, my hat. I always forget my hat.

Mother: I am glad you remembered it this time.

Son: And can you be sure to grab me a snack for after school?

Mother: Of course.

In this example, the parent needed to provide fewer prompts than for the preschool-aged child. As children get older, they often possess the knowledge needed to formulate a plan, but they must practice their planning skills. The parent of a school-aged child can facilitate forward thinking by drawing out the conversation and by helping the child reflect on the situation. Whenever possible, practice planning in the context of your child's area of interest, because children are more likely to think deeply about things that captivate them. Your child's plans should be a frequent topic of discussion. "How much time do you need to get ready?" "What are you going to do after school?" "When do you plan to do your homework?" "I am going grocery shopping, so do you want me to buy anything special for dinner this week?" and "What do you want in your lunch?" are examples of the many types of planning conversations that can take place every day.

Allowance for chores can be used to encourage planning, but be careful: if rewards are not used properly, they can cause problems. Allowance rewards effort, and money provides the opportunity for a child to save and plan. Encourage your child to save at least a portion of his earnings for something he wants, or may want, at a later time. In our family, we highlight saving by offering a "matching gift." We tell our children that if they put a portion of their allowance into the bank, at the end of the year we will double what they have saved. Because they usually opt to save their money, we have the opportunity to discuss planning for a goal. Within reason, encourage your child to spend his money how he wants. Help him keep his fiscal goal in mind by either storing change in a clear jar so that he can see progress or counting down until he reaches his goal. When the idea of allowance is not done properly, giving your child money can actually dis-incentivize effort. What you don't want is a child who refuses to work unless you pay him. My suggestion is to make it clear that allowance is for "extra help" around the house. It is expected that your child, depending on his age, will do some work (eg, clean up after himself) simply because he lives there. If he does not help around the house, allowance is not given for the extra work. If you give too much allowance or buy him unnecessary toys, your child will not value the effort required to earn what one wants. Allowance, when administered judiciously, is a useful incentive, and, more important, the money earned is an effective tool for teaching your child to plan ahead.

Toys and activities can promote planning (Box 6-7). Building toys such as Lego bricks, K'nex sets, and blocks encourage children to make mental blueprints of what they want to create. Just like when an architect makes a plan while designing a building, these mental blueprints are your child's planning skills at work. Some games can also require children to plan. Strategy games such as chess, checkers, and Connect Four are good examples of games that encourage forward thinking. Very few electronic games encourage planning to the same degree as many classic strategy games. Electronic games usually lead players through the activity. The planning and creativity is often done for them, by the clever people who designed the game. The act of playing a musical instrument demands simultaneous processing (reading music and planning motor movements) and likely has a positive impact on the development of forward-thinking skills. Last, as mentioned in the previous chapter, Chapter 5, Raising an Organized Preschooler, activities that encourage imagination also support the growth of planning skills.

Box 6-7

Examples of Games That Promote Planning

Mastermind	Mancala
Blokus	Backgammon
Chess	Pictionary
Balderdash	Khet
Cranium	

Summarizing

An older school-aged child should be able to summarize, an important simultaneous processing skill. To make a summary statement, the child not only needs to remember an event, but also to consider what is most important about that event, in order to formulate an efficient statement. Parents can promote this skill by asking their child about what is going on in her life: ask about sporting events, shows watched, games played, and activities with friends, for example. My children know that when they go to a movie with their friends, my wife and I will ask them to give us a summary when they return to home.

Sometimes, students who have trouble giving a verbal summary need other ways to summarize their thoughts. One year when I was coaching a fifth grade all-star basketball team, I encountered such a student. At our first team practice, I gathered all the best players from several teams in our league and I asked them one at a time to describe the most effective play used by their former team. One player struggled with this task. Noting the confusion on the faces of the other players and having no clue myself what he was talking about, I asked him to draw the play on my coaching whiteboard. His illustration clearly summarized the play. Later, his parents confided in me that he had an auditory processing disorder that made it difficult for him to organize his thoughts into words, and they were relieved to know that we were using picture plans to reinforce our verbal instructions.

School-aged children are capable of setting goals, making plans, and summarizing and should be encouraged to do so. Encourage your child to take on responsibilities, and try not to be overprotective. Have your child unplug and play, because play provides many opportunities to plan. At first, they may need scaffolding to remind them about the steps needed to complete tasks. But remember that practice makes permanent, so it is important that your child has the opportunity to practice and learn.

Recommendations for Forward Thinking in School-aged Children

Planning

- Use conversation to co-construct plans and help your child with forward thinking. Encourage your child to plan by drawing out the conversation and then reflecting on your child's comments.

- Bring forward thinking to your child's conscious by reflecting on mistakes, such as "Was that a helpful choice or an unhelpful choice?" Then ask your child to plan for the future, such as "What could you do next time?" Try to remain calm, because expressing your anger at your child's impulsive behavior often makes the situation worse, and sometimes it can deflect from a learning opportunity.

- Play games that promote planning.
- Encourage your children to cook and bake. Parental supervision will be required for your younger bakers. Children can prepare their own breakfast by early elementary school (eg, cereal, toast, oatmeal) and, once they are safe to do so, more-elaborate meals (eg, eggs and pancakes) by middle school.
- Encourage your children to learn to play a musical instrument.
- Provide homework support that is commensurate with your child's needs. Teach your child to make a plan for homework (eg, prioritize, allocate time), collect materials for the first step, set a time goal and use a timer, complete the first, put completed work into a backpack compartment, collect materials for the second step, and proceed in the same way. Remember, parents should look for opportunities to remove themselves from the homework process.
- By providing models and examples of successful work from previous years, teachers can help children envision a plan for their own successful project. Draw students' attention to specific qualities of the work and show students the plans that were used to complete projects to aid in connecting a plan to a completed assignment.
- Long-term projects at school can provide students with great practice at many organizational skills. Encourage your child to begin planning and completing big assignments on his or her own. In class, teachers can emphasize time management, talk about budgeting time, and give students sufficient notice regarding tests and other deadlines. They can help students plan their time allocation and schedule for each part of a specific project. The activities can be designed such that students have to demonstrate good planning and time management, along with effective organization of materials needed for the project.

- Discuss being prepared for tasks. Planning should include time and material management.

- Introduce an allowance and encourage your child to set financial goals with his newfound wealth. If your child wants to make a large purchase, you can encourage him to work for and save money for the purpose. You can apply this to many things, including clothes, shoes, and a bike, especially if he insists on wanting items more expensive than you want to pay for.

- Encourage your child to become increasingly independent by allowing her to arrange her own playdates and to think of ideas and activities to do with friends.

- Parents can also give their school-aged child the opportunity to make a variety of fun plans. One perfect annual activity for kids is to plan their birthday party. Parents can guide the planning and assist their children to make sure that they consider important details, such as who to invite, logistics, menu, and activities to do and games to play. Children can also practice planning their valentines to classmates, holiday presents to make or buy for family and friends, what to be for Halloween, and more. Most kids love to take on more and more ownership of this type of plan creation.

Estimating

- Students should practice estimation when performing math. Encourage your child to predict the answer before solving a problem.

- Encourage your child to note the time it takes to accomplish a certain task, in order to help with estimating and allocating time for future planned activities (eg, practicing guitar, studying for an English test). Let your child estimate how long tasks will take. Documenting these aspects can help make your child more aware of time, and organization, and provide him better feedback. Before he goes to bed, have your child check off his accomplishments and document how long each took to complete. When a discrepancy exists between the estimate and the actual time, encourage your child to consider why this occurred.

■ Encourage your child to make estimations about time or amounts; for example, when taking a car ride, ask your child to predict how long it will take to arrive at the destination. If this task is difficult for your child, provide scaffolding by reminding your child of related information your child likely already knows.

Predicting

■ Read stories with your school-aged child, and while you're at it, encourage your school-aged child to make predictions about stories. Preview each book with her by looking at the cover, as well as chapter titles. Share your prior knowledge about the book topic.

Summarizing

■ After reading a chapter, stop and ask your child to summarize what it was about and then provide your take on the chapter.

■ There are many opportunities to help develop summarization skills. When your child goes somewhere without you, ask him to tell about what he did. Ask for an overview from your child after he reads a book or watches a movie.

■ Use conversation at dinnertime to encourage your child to tell about the day. Sometimes children need help starting a summary. Young children can be prompted to tell a highlight, a lowlight, and something funny as a framework. Parents can also model how to share by summarizing their own days.

Step 5: Promote problem-solving

The school-age years should be a time of tremendous growth as children explore new situations. A school-aged child discovers interests such as sports, dance, chess, reading, animals, and being an "A" student. Exploring new interests prompts your child to solve new problems. Participation in group activities (eg, drama, sports, scouting) and the greater academic demands placed onto a school-aged child encourage time management, material management, and social and cognitive processing (the brain's process of acquiring knowledge though thoughts, experiences, and senses). During the school-age years, your child will most likely grow from needing homework supervision to managing his own work. He will spend increasing amounts of time with friends and at sleepovers that are outside of your supervision. During this period, children start to earn freedoms. By the time your child hits middle school, you may feel comfortable leaving him at home for extended periods. With this freedom, school-aged children can sometimes make mistakes. Remember that mistakes are part of growing up, and the act of fixing the problem is a valuable exercise for your child. An organized student is a good problem-solver, and your guidance will play a big role in your child's emerging independence. Encourage your child to be increasingly independent before you step in and rescue him.

Students' problem-solving skills are emerging, but not fully developed. I remember participating on a swim team during the summers of my childhood. When I was 11, I noticed that the top older swimmers would "shave down" (shave their body hair to reduce drag) before the championship meet. Wanting a good result, I decided that if it worked for those hairy teens, it would also work for "peach fuzz" me. So when my parents went out that evening before the big race, I decided to shave my legs. Using my mom's razor and no lubricant, I proceeded to cut up my legs. Now it may have been a good idea to shave my legs, but why wouldn't have I asked my parents for help? Why would school-aged me use a razor for the first time when nobody else was home? The answer is that my problem-solving skills were emerging, but I did not quite yet grasp the big picture.

Big Picture

As your child gets older, he will become more capable of seeing the big picture, a skill that is found in all organized thinkers. A mature school-aged child makes good choices about his time, is prepared for his activities, respects the opinions of others, and independently makes sound decisions based on all the information available to him. Seeing the big picture is comparable to stepping back and looking at the entirety of a famous painting. While a close-up view of the artwork may tell something about the color or the type of brushstroke, this view tells nothing about the meaning, expression, or emotions of the painting. A good problem-solver considers all the evidence and to do so requires the ability to simultaneously process multiple data points. School-aged children who lack problem-solving skills can be very "right and wrong" on issues. They are often rule followers and become frustrated by uncertainty or when others stray from their expected paths. They demonstrate limited insight into the thoughts, feelings, and opinions of others. Socially, this may result in conflicts or peer avoidance. Academically, there may be misinterpretations about teacher expectations. Clearly, it is important to teach your school-aged child to practice problem-solving so that your child can learn to see the big picture. Modeling the behavior is the best way to teach this lesson to your child. Be careful to listen to your child and others. Avoid rushing into a response. Consider all options before making a conclusion.

Imagination

The best practice field for problem-solving is the imagination, as has been discussed in previous sections of this book. Through creative play, a child can exercise his simultaneous processing and problem-solving skills. Pretend play provides your child with a variety of problems to solve. Whether it's 2 children wanting to play the same role or 2 children searching for the just-right material to make a roof for the playhouse, your child calls on important thinking skills that he will use in every aspect of his life, now and forever. A creative child should be able play out multiple different options for any given scenario. While kindergartners understand the difference between what is real and what is pretend, allowing imaginative play to be even more fun and silly, the attention and sequencing skills of school-aged children are greater so that they can carry out long and detailed scenarios. Rehearse role-playing and social stories with children who do not demonstrate creativity, and give all children the opportunity and encouragement to use their imagination.

Children can also practice their problem-solving skills in creative ways. I love playmaking as a great problem-solving challenge. The problem could be "How can we put on our own version of Pinocchio?" The kids then need to think about props and costumes. You can support this play by having bins of dress-up materials. The children can work together to plan out the performance and assign roles to each other. Parents can share books about Pinocchio that range from comical to historical and can help analyze characters. In total, the playmaking experience can be a tremendous learning and problem-solving adventure.

Benefits Gained From Imaginative Play

- Imagination helps school-aged children solve problems by helping them think through different outcomes to various situations and role-play ways to cope with difficult or new circumstances.

- Imagination allows children to practice real-life skills. From shopping at a pretend grocery store to assigning roles and dialogue to dolls or puppets, children's pretend play helps them practice and apply new learning and better understand how those skills are used in the real world.

- Imagination encourages a rich vocabulary. Telling and hearing real or made-up stories, reading books, and pretend play help children learn and retain new words.

- Imagination helps children grow up to be adults who are creative thinkers. Adults who were imaginative children often become problem-solvers, innovators, and creative thinkers.

The more basic toys foster creativity. Take a Barbie doll, for instance, which used to be available as only a few doll options and children could pretend it was a lawyer or a pilot. Today, we have a plethora of doll options, including Barbie dolls who are flight attendants, doctors, veterinarians, teachers, and more—in some ways, the vast variety of toys actually discourages using imagination. Do not feel compelled to purchase the latest fad or sophisticated electronics. Keep it simple and enjoy building and creating.

Summarization

Your greatest opportunity to promote problem-solving in your child will be through conversations. In our family, we use dinnertime as an opportunity to practice summarizing. All 7 of us get the opportunity to talk about our day. My wife and I model a clear summary of our days. We simplify the task for young children. They are asked to tell about a high point, a low point, and something funny that happened. The older kids give a topic sentence ("Today was a good day, or a sad day, or a scary day") and support it with explanations.

How we use our words is a window to our organizational skills. A well-organized summary reflects not only a perspective of the listener's interest but also a solid grasp of the big picture. A concise summary illustrates the most important points and generally has a clear topic sentence, but it does not get bogged down into a play-by-play of everything that happened. It is very common for school-aged children to ramble, but you want to encourage your child to be concise. When your child's conversation is tangential, try to summarize what he said to show your understanding, thereby modeling a good summary. Personally, I appreciate the technique that when speaking or writing, one should (a) tell people what you are going to say, (b) say it, and (c) tell them what was said.

Be an active listener to your school-aged child so that he will want to share with you his thoughts. Active listening means asking questions and reflecting on what he says. It does not mean solving your child's problem for him or correcting every inaccuracy, because that gets frustrating to kids and, frankly, it gets frustrating to adults too. Instead, when you disagree or when something your child says does not make sense, try challenging him to clarify (eg, "I don't understand how your teacher wants the book report to look when it gets turned in" or "Can you explain that to me again, because I didn't get the part about how you went from losing the game to being the best player on the field?"). By admitting that you do not understand something, you give your child the chance to either explain himself more thoroughly or rethink his logic, without making your child feel threatened that he did something wrong.

Flexible Thinking

In turn, you can share your personal dilemmas with your child. You can model your flexible thinking for your child. Let your child know how you sorted through a work problem. When scheduling conflicts occur, share them with your school-aged child and ask for his opinion, and then explain your logic behind the decision you make to create a solution. Learning to work together to solve problems is a valuable skill for a school-aged child who is navigating the social hierarchy of elementary and middle school. Collaborative problem-solving, nicely described by Ross Greene in his book *The Explosive Child,* is a valuable skill to learn, but it demands perspective taking and flexible thinking. When performed correctly, this skill can help your child avoid frustrations.

For instance, getting dressed in time for school can be an ongoing battle for parents and kids. Here is one family's story. The mother reported that each morning is a confrontation at their home. Her 8-year-old, she reported, "is always running behind, and when I pick out her clothes for her, she tells me they are ugly and refuses to wear them." I suggested that she let her daughter pick out the clothes, but the daughter claimed that she does not have time in the morning—and this statement caused a sudden outburst from the mom about how the child dillydallies in the morning. Scolding a child almost never helps. When I redirected the conversation, I asked the mother what she really wants each day. The answer was for the child to get ready faster in the morning. I then asked the child what she wants, and she said that she wants to pick out her own clothes, but she doesn't have enough time. I framed the dilemma, "How could you give yourself more time to get ready so that your mother could leave you alone in the morning?" On her own, the little girl suggested that she could pick out her clothes the night before so that they were ready when she woke up. Notice the difference between collaborative problem-solving and compromising? In collaborative problem-solving, we teach the child that she can give you what you want (in this case, it was to get ready on time), but she can also find a way to get what she wants (to pick out her own clothes). In a compromise, both would be giving something, such as she could leave late to school, but that would not be an adequate solution. Compromise is important at times, but collaborative problem-solving is a much more powerful tool for flexible thinking.

Perspective Taking

The art of collaborative problem-solving requires good social perspective taking, because in order to make a compromise, one needs to understand the wants and needs of her partner. Consider 2 third graders playing on the playground together at recess. One child suggests playing "Hot Lava Monster." The second child says, "We always play Hot Lava Monster. That game is stupid." Child number 1 can at that point (a) call child number 2 stupid, pick up tanbark, and throw it at his face or (b) find a solution. To solve this problem, he needs to first figure out what child 2 wants to play, such as "I really like Hot Lava Monster, but what do you want to play?" Child 2 considers his options and then says, "Freeze Tag." "Great," says child number 1, "I like Freeze Tag too. Let's play Freeze Tag this recess and Hot Lava Monster next recess." Problem solved. Both kids got what they wanted and conflicts were avoided. It takes years to learn perspective taking and collaborative problem-solving skills. Your job is to promote opportunities for your child to practice this skill. This means your child should play with his peers or as we now call it, have playdates. Unstructured playdates are also important, because there are more opportunities for problems to occur that need to be solved. Since it seems that very few children these days have the opportunity to go next door and play with other kids, you may need to schedule unstructured playdates for your child, or better yet, suggest a playdate and have your child plan it.

Teach your child to be a good friend. Discuss the components of friendship: sharing interests and anticipating needs, wants, and feelings. Friends do nice things for each other and so encourage your children to think about ways to make their friends happy and not just to care for themselves. Your younger school-aged child will still be working on sharing and turn taking, but he may occasionally be proactively thoughtful about a friend. For example, he may ask for a second treat that he can give to his friend later. Your older elementary school child will be learning how to negotiate peace treaties that allow both he and his friend to get what they want. Your middle school-aged children will be spontaneously doing nice things for their friends. They will write nice notes to them or pay them compliments. They may think about birthday gifts or other niceties that will make their friend happy. Friendship skills vary greatly from child to child and so some 8-year-olds are giving gifts to their friends, while some tweens are still learning to share. Since so much variability exists in social ability, it is difficult to assign specific benchmarks, but as parents, recognize that you can promote perspective taking by encouraging your child to build friendships.

Dealing With Boredom

While playdates are great, remember that boredom is also a positive driving force, because boredom in itself is a dilemma for your child to solve. A bored child must solve the problem "What can I do?" So, when friends are not available to play, avoid letting your child default to television or the computer. Instead, let boredom drive his creative play. I am afraid that school-aged children stop being creative and silly too early these days, because their need to use these skills is compromised by the availability of technology. Too often we as parents feel compelled to rescue our children from boredom by allowing them to have an iPad in a restaurant, sitting them in front of the television to keep them occupied, or overscheduling their after-school time. Instead, you can give some suggestions and let your child try to figure out some fun for himself.

To reduce students' chances for experiencing boredom, they can practice creating mental lists of things to do, for example, when it rains on a weekend or for when it is time to turn off the television set. When your child is in a good mood, try to brainstorm and problem-solve ideas for the next time your child says, "There's nothing to do." Give him some general parameters and ideas, or suggest creating lists of options and activities. A very organized thinker will access his mental drop-down menu of things that he had wanted to do earlier, but didn't have time for, or his menu of things that have been fun during past similarly boring situations. A creative thinker may invent new games or stories to pass the time.

To aid your child's efforts to occupy himself, keep art, craft, and building supplies available so that he can sit down and do a project or go outside to build and create. Have musical instruments handy for him to try and practice playing. When he does invent, support the creativity more than you talk about the mess—promoting your child's problem-solving skills in this way is critical to developing his organized thinking.

Teaching Problem-solving to School-aged Students

Problem-solving

- Encourage independence. Allow your child the opportunity to develop age-appropriate skills such as showering, going to bed on his own, managing homework, and, when ready, staying home alone.
- Challenge your child to do new things. New activities, such as teams, clubs, and groups, provide unique challenges as your child tries to navigate the social and unwritten expectations of the group.

■ Allow your child to struggle through difficult situations that your child can handle. Avoid rescuing your child or making things too easy by doing too much for your child.

Imagination

■ Acknowledge and support your child's efforts to be creative and model creativity yourself. For instance, instead of going to an arcade (eg, Chuck E. Cheese's) for a birthday party, try creating fun games and activities to host at home.

■ There are many imaginative options to expand your child's horizons; try craft making, science kits, and magic sets.

Dealing With Boredom

■ Allow your children to have free time and be bored, and learn to deal with gaps in their schedule. If boredom is an insurmountable obstacle for your children—they have difficulty accessing their mental file of fun activities— you can scaffold this task. When you and your child are in a good mood, sit down and make lists of things your child likes to do when, for instance, it is raining or he has a friend over, or things he can play in the backyard. Then when he is bored, refer him to his own list of appropriate ideas.

■ Limit access to electronics, as those activities generally require minimal creativity.

Flexible Thinking

■ Practice collaborative problem-solving when compliance is an issue because your child is stuck. Empathize with him. Help him frame the dilemma (eg, "How do I give him what he wants and still get some of what I want?"). Invite him to solve the problem. Remember that this is not compromising; it is problem-solving.

■ Discuss flexible thinking and acknowledge your child for shifting smoothly from one perspective to the next. For children who have very inflexible behavior, you must provide them with a warning of an upcoming change in plans. A ticket system can be used for unexpected change. A parent can hand them a "ticket" as a warning that a change is about to occur. Two minutes later, the parent can discuss the change in plans. If the child copes smoothly with the change, the ticket can be turned in at bedtime for a small reward.

Language of Problem-solving

■ Discuss idioms with your school-aged child to see whether he can interpret the double meanings. For example, "fish out of water," "icing on the cake," or "play it by ear."

■ Parents and teachers can discuss analogies and metaphors to encourage students to develop their complex thinking.

Summarizing

■ Encourage your school-aged student to summarize. Be patient and listen to his explanations. Model consistent summarization. Remember the rule: tell people what you are going to say, say it, and tell them what was said. When your child rambles or is tangential, tell him that you are confused and ask a question to help him focus his response.

Perspective Taking

■ Talk about the feelings of other children. When out in public, make observations to your child about other children using the emotions they express. Point out when your child does something to make you or someone else feel happy.

■ Continue discussing the perspectives of others. School-aged children can discuss peer preferences. Middle school and teenaged students can be encouraged to take the viewpoints of adults.

■ Give your child the opportunity to interact with peers. At first, interactions can be brief and focused on targeted activities, such as going to the park or the library with a friend. As children develop their social cognition, they can have playdates to practice being social, but at first, limit the length of these playdates so that they end on a positive note. Group play can be more difficult. Gradually ease your young child into group play activities.

■ Teach your child about making friends. Help her realize that friendships require shared experiences, common interests, thinking about the other person's interests, and making efforts to make your friends happy by anticipating their needs, hopes, and goals.

Transitioning Tips

■ Parents and teachers can prepare students for transitions by using schedules, routines, warnings, and previewing strategies.

■ To help children who have transitional challenges learn to initiate tasks, parents and teacher may need to build getting started into activities by creating timelines that include initiating tasks.

■ Discuss transitions with your child, and acknowledge when your child shifts smoothly from one task to the next.

■ Children transition better when their schedules are predictable. For a child who lacks organization, set a specific routine for starting the day, which involves a preview of what he can expect throughout the day. Once the routine is comfortable, gradually introduce variations.

■ Teachers can improve flexible behavior in their students by making the school routine and environment predictable.

■ Rules should be clearly displayed and consistently enforced.

■ Schedules and assignments should be posted daily.

■ Attention should be called to schedule changes.

■ Warning should be given before making a change to the classroom, such as a new seating arrangement.

Chapter 7

Raising an Organized Teenager: Preparing for Launch

So your child is growing up, and as she gets more mature, your role as a parent changes from being a coach during the school-age period and a manager during middle school to now evolving into more of a consultant. A consultant is there to help when a request is made or when a problem arises. A middle school student needs a moderate amount of guidance, but a successful teen who has been given a set of clear rules and boundaries can operate much more independently. Mature teens can be trusted to stay home alone for increasing amounts of time, they can track their own grades and homework, and many will soon be getting their driver's permit. A responsible teen can be trusted to hang out with friends and stay out of trouble. Parents should pay attention to 2 considerations when it comes to their teenagers: (1) Are they giving their teen enough space so that he can grow into an independent adult? and (2) Do they have a mature teen? Remember that age and development are 2 different things. Just because someone hits 13 or 14 years old physically does not mean that he is mentally at that level. Some teens, especially young teens, need more management than others. In doing so, be respectful, be consistent, and demonstrate why some assistance makes sense.

The teenage years are full of emotional turmoil and change. The hormonal changes that teenagers experience heightens every emotion: funny is funnier, anger is angrier, sadness is sadder, and silliness is sillier. Meanwhile, it seems as if everything in the life of a teenager is changing. Their bodies grow taller, get muscular or curvier, and even get hairier. They start high school and friend groups change. Homework increases in amount and can be more challenging . They go to football games and dances. And eventually, they start driving and many even find a job. And yes, some teens start dating. Things are changing for teens, and yet not every teen is yet developmentally prepared for these changes.

It is important to know what your teen can and cannot do, and the best way to find this out is to give her the independence to try age-appropriate tasks. By the time your child is a teenager, she should be more independent than dependent. Most teenagers can wake themselves up and get themselves ready for school on time. They can prepare meals and they have their own social life. And while they are more skilled, the demands placed onto them dramatically increase. At school, they have more classes during which notetaking is required and teachers who expect them to complete projects with far-off due dates. In high school, teachers stop giving timelines and expect teens to manage their own time. In addition to their school responsibilities, teens are having to balance their extracurricular activities and their expanding social lives. While consistent parenting will not eliminate the ups and downs of adolescence, it can make life more predictable and reassuring for a growing teen.

Step 1: Be consistent

Consistent Structure

Parents should not only be consistent about expectations and rules but also be consistent with their emotional state, because many teens will struggle to keep their emotions in check. Like children of all ages, teenagers respond best to consistent parents, but unlike with younger children, the immediate ramifications of inconsistent parenting of teens can be more dangerous. For example, parents who send mixed messages or do not model positive behavior about texting and driving, teenage drinking, or smoking could be setting themselves up for an unexpected party when they leave the house.

Teenagers will test everyone's limits, including their own, and in the absence of structure, they will often make choices that are not in their best interest. There are foundational boundaries that are necessary for their health: sleep, exercise, and nutrition. These are the same issues that were critical for infants and toddlers, but for teenagers, they take on a different significance. Teenagers need to perform, for instance, at sports, or in school clubs, or academically, for all their many classes and big exams, and when they do not take care of themselves, they tend to underachieve. Further, the foundational habits teens develop will likely follow them to college, when you can no longer supervise your teen, making it even more critical to emphasize consistency around these boundaries. But how does a parent set limits for a teen who does not like to be told what to do? Instead of telling your son what to eat, insist that he eats dinner with the family and then serve a healthy dinner. You can avoid some arguments over bedtimes by setting limits on screen time, such as no cell phones, iPads, or electronics after 9:00 pm (and model that as parents), so that there is not much for him to do in the evening other than go to bed. Another way to prevent your teen from staying up too late is to limit his sleeping in on the weekends. If the family gets up and does chores, goes jogging, goes to church, or visits the farmer's market together at 9:00 am, he will have to go to bed earlier. Whatever strategy you choose, do it consistently.

Teenagers often want to know why they have to follow a certain rule, but parents do not want to have to constantly explain themselves. By being consistent about rules that emphasize the big picture, repetitive explanations are often not required because the rules make sense. For instance, one of the ways I explain curfew to my teens is I tell them that "bad things can happen after midnight." When incidents occur, I take time to talk to my kids about the newspaper articles. We talk about the drunk drivers or the poor decisions made by teens that have led to crashes or injuries, which always seem to happen late at night. I try to make a point that there is no reason to be out that late, and when people get tired, their judgment is compromised. I have also seen the parents of my patients successfully emphasize the benefits of a B average by showing their teen the different cost of car insurance for a B average student and C average student. By consistently emphasizing rules that reflect on the big picture, parents can avoid using potentially argumentative and maddening statements like "Because I said so."

Consistent Emotion

Teens will occasionally make mistakes, and the consistent way to respond to their indiscretions is by showing them the natural consequences of their actions, not necessarily by punishing them. Punishment is usually met with anger and resistance. For example, if a teenager is not being a safe driver, parents should not let him drive, because the big picture is that it is a parent's job to keep his or her teen safe. If the teen is not demonstrating the maturity needed to drive safely by listening to the radio too loud, not using a seat belt, or having multiple friends in his car at one time, the natural consequence is that he is not given the opportunity to drive until he demonstrates more maturity. Punishing the student by telling him he cannot go out for 1 month for a driving offense is off target. In fact, it might be good to let him go out and deal with the frustration, embarrassment, and natural consequences of not being able to drive for a month.

During the teen years, your student will seek independence and grapple with establishing his identity. This transformation happens amidst surges in hormone levels, and these hormonal changes can wreak havoc on emotions. Now, many of us have negative associations with the emotions of a teenager, but being a teenager can be really fun; it is like riding a roller coaster with ups and downs and unexpected turns. I miss some of the revelry I experienced when I was a teen. It would be great, as an adult, to be able to sit in the back seat of a car with your buddies and laugh hysterically at fart jokes for an entire 30-minute car ride. Teens are disinhibited, and along with the floods of laughter come sudden and intense sadness and anger. Given that teens will likely be emotionally unstable, it is even more important that parents demonstrate emotional self-control during stressful situations. When your teen is overreacting to a situation, remember to maintain calm. Avoid any yelling matches. As a parent of 5 wonderful and strong-willed children, I know how difficult this can be, and I have found that it helps to remind myself of a few principles.

- All people want to feel accepted and not judged. This principle is especially important for a teen, because at this developmental stage, teens are trying to establish their identity and where they fit in.
- Stay focused on the big picture. It is very easy to get sidetracked by seemingly illogical and irrational statements that teens can make during an argument. Sometimes they even resort to name-calling and foul language. That issue can be dealt with later, in a more calm and rational moment (although it is OK to point it out, such as "Let's avoid name-calling"); during the disagreement, stick to the big picture.
- Find common ground; for example, say things like "You and I both want you to do well on your test," "My biggest concern is your safety," or "You have had problems with your health when you stay up late."
- BE CONSISTENT. Now more than ever, teens need consistent rules, limits, and boundaries.

Consistency Recommendations for Teenagers

Consistent Structure

- Rules (eg, curfew, electronic limits) should be made very clear to your teenager and put into place to emphasize the big picture, and then these rules should be consistently reinforced.

- Expect that your teen regularly perform chores so that he can learn responsibility and how to balance school, social, and home lives.

- Emphasize the foundational principles of health (sleep, exercise, and nutrition), education, and helping the family (chores).

- Let a mature teenager know that as long as he meets his obligations, he has freedom to make choices about how he spends his time.

- Avoid punishment, but use natural consequences.

- Do not undermine societal rules and laws by breaking them in front of your teen, for example, running a red light, texting and driving, telling a white lie, or calling in sick when you are not. A respect for laws and rules may help keep your teenager safe when he is on he own.

- Most teenagers should be fairly independent by the time they reach 18 years of age. To prepare them for their independence, the parent role should change during the teen years from being a manager to becoming a consultant who is available when your teen has a question.

- Maintain a consistent emotion when responding during disagreements and stressful situations.

Step 2: Introduce order

The teenage years are a transformative period for both parents and teenagers. A major parenting goal is to get your teen ready for college by age 18. Accomplishing this milestone requires both growth in independence for the teen and a letting go of control by the parent, which is a subtle balancing act. Parents do not want to give up control too soon and cause their teen to struggle with the consequences of too much independence, but they also do not want to be too controlling to the point that their teen's development is stifled.

Raul graduated from high school with a 4.1 GPA and was accepted to a prestigious college. However, he made it through high school with too much parental support. During high school, his parents spent 5 hours per night assisting with homework completion. When assignments went missing, his parents would call the high school teachers. So much effort was put toward homework that he did not participate in school activities or develop friendships. Three months into his college, his parents learned that he had been skipping class and earning failing grades. His father moved into his dorm room, literally sleeping on his floor, between the 2 roommates, 3 days per week to ensure that Raul would wake up on time and make it to class. Unprepared to schedule and develop his own routines, he returned home without completing a year of college.

Sadly, I have met a number of families in which the teenager, with tremendous help from his parents, earned high marks in high school and was accepted to a prestigious college only to fail out in the first year because he could not manage his own time. Time that should have been spent studying was used up with gaming. A parent's role during the middle and late teen years is to act as a consultant, and the teen's job, at least at first, is to consult regularly (eg, "Can I stay out until 11:00 pm?" "Can I go to the movie with John?" or "Can you look at the conclusion of my essay?") By the late teen years, these consultations should be less frequent, but still occasionally needed, even by college students (eg, "What should I ask in my job interview?" or "How should I handle a roommate issue?").

Time Management

The sequential skills to focus on during the teen years are time management and becoming a "closer." Homework challenges both of these skills; students need to track assignments and turn in the finished product on time. Younger teens may need some reminders to complete their work, but older teens should learn to operate independently. (Refer to Box 6-6 in the previous chapter, Raising an Organized School-aged Child, to see the different levels of parental homework intervention.) Teens often resist prompting and encouragement from their parents, but they are more receptive to support from a tutor, a teacher, or an older student. If you are fortunate enough to have a teen who will listen to your advice, be careful not to overstep your boundaries by managing his assignments. Instead, help him set up tracking systems such as calendars and assignment books or teach him to use routines such as regularly looking at the online scheduling tool that his school may use. Teaching good habits and management routines will be very valuable to your teen in the long run.

Parents can promote the development of temporal awareness in teens by giving deadlines that apply to everyday life. These deadlines promote an awareness of time, for example, "The trash needs to be taken to the curb by dark," "Have the table set by 5:00 pm," or "Be home by 10:00 pm." Establishing deadlines allows students to practice managing their own time on tasks that are less critical than homework assignments and term papers.

Students who struggle with meeting deadlines should practice "backward time planning." This method of organizing begins with a goal, such as going to bed by 10:00 pm, and then projecting backward. Brushing teeth: 5 minutes, 9:55. Shower: 20 minutes, 9:35. Watch a show: 30 minutes, 9:05. Prep backpack for the next day: 10 minutes, 8:55. Math homework: 60 minutes, 7:55. English homework: 30 minutes plus 10-minute break, 7:15. Dinner and cleanup: 45 minutes, 6:30. History homework: 45 minutes, 5:45. This exercise can show how a student can get homework done, go to bed on time, and still have about 3 hours of after-school time for sports or other entertainment. Some kids like to adjust the schedule to have longer breaks later in the evening. Others, like those taking attention medications that wear off earlier in the day, like to start their homework schedule when they get home from school so that they can have more free time later in the evening. The key is to start at the deadline and work backward.

You can continue to support your teenager by sticking to schedules. Establishing routines becomes more complicated with after-school activities, more-mature friendships, and the freedom that comes with driving. Yet, teaching the value of a schedule continues to be an important life lesson. Try to have regular times for dinner, family meetings, curfews, electronic blackouts, and other family rituals to reinforce the concept of deadlines. Sharing an online family calendar can inform your teen about life events such as doctor visits, responsibilities, and vacations, while modeling good organizational skills.

"Closing"

"Closing" is an extremely useful skill for a student to master before heading off to college. Again, closing is the ability to be thorough when completing a project—completion is the last step in a sequence. Teach your teen that whatever task she does, it should be done well and to completion. This skill will be important not only in college but also in life. Some commonly encountered situations during which teenagers can learn to be comprehensive include tidying the kitchen after preparing a meal or folding and putting away washed clothes. These skills translate to being thorough with schoolwork, such as making sure essays are edited, tests are double-checked, and work is turned in on time.

Start training your teen for independence by giving her ownership of tasks. By the end of high school, a teenager should be able to complete a task from start to finish. Foster this skill by assigning her manageable tasks such as putting together an unassembled desk or preparing meals. Remember that finishing tasks includes cleaning up. Never forget to compliment your teenager when she shows the independence or responsibility needed to complete a project. Eventually, your teen will make the connection that completing one type of project (such as preparing a meal) translates to school and work.

 Sequencing Recommendations for Teenagers

Time Management

- Instead of micromanaging your teen's activities, try setting up systems to help him be more successful on his own, such as calendar tools on his phone and assisting with list making.
- Calendars should be used to help keep track of appointments, practices, and deadlines, as well as family expectations. As a student progress

through high school, he should be expected to maintain his own calendar, while still having access to a shared family calendar, if needed.

- Encourage participation in family responsibilities (eg, following instructions to assemble a new piece of furniture, doing laundry, washing cars, or cooking a meal).
- Deadlines help teach the significance of time management. Give deadlines for everyday tasks (eg, room cleaned by noon, being home by 6:00 pm).
- Master "backward time planning." In other words, if you have to be doing something, somewhere at 5:00 pm, at what time do you need to begin to do the other steps you need to complete (eg, finishing homework, getting dressed, packing any gear) in order to be ready to go and get there on time, while allowing for possibilities such as traffic or finding parking.

"Closing"

- Make sure that your teen can take a project from start to finish. Emphasize the importance of completing a project by, for instance, encouraging editing and reminding about cleanup.

"Step Wisdom"

- Continue to be consistent with limit setting. Remember that cause and effect is the most basic sequence. Therefore, natural consequences for a student's actions are an important way to emphasize a fundamental of sequential organization.

Life Skills for Your Teen

- Before your teen heads off to college, it is important that your teen has the ability to perform at least the following reasonable household skills, which are needed for independent living:
- Makes bed daily
- Changes bed linens regularly
- Does laundry and puts his clean clothes into his dresser or closet

- Takes out trash as needed and replaces trash can liners
- Recycles in appropriate containers
- Sweeps and mops floors and vacuums carpets
- Cleans shower to prevent soap scum and mildew
- Is able to use a plunger to fix a toilet
- Adjusts thermostat and lights to conserve energy when leaving
- Can change light bulbs and batteries
- Can be fiscally responsible with an allowance and manage his own checking and savings accounts
- Knows how to prepare some basic meals

Step 3: Give everything a place

The principle of giving everything a place remains the same for a teen as it did for when she was a school-aged child, but the stakes are higher. Teens will still need to clean up and manage their materials, but now they are also tracking high-value items. Teens need to track their identification, wallets, car keys, homework, and often portable electronics, such as phones, tablets, and laptops.

When I started driving, I would frequently misplace my car keys. It would have been smart to solve this problem by attaching my keys to a belt hook or carefully checking my pockets before leaving a room. However, at 16 my solution was to hide a hanger under my rear bumper. This worked. When my keys were missing, I would pull out the hanger, feed it through the space above the driver side window, and unlock the door. Then I would use the spare key under the mat of my burgundy station wagon to drive home. When I married my wife, she gave me a small basket that we keep near the front door. In 25 years of marriage, I have never misplaced my keys. "Give everything a place" is an important lesson for all of us and is way easier than using a hanger to break into one's car.

By the time your child reaches her teen years, she will most likely have acquired the visual processing abilities (abilities to make sense of information taken in through the eyes) needed to be organized. The focus thus shifts from exercising the brain to mastering skills. Teenagers must learn to be responsible; for spatial organization, that means keeping track of possessions and being neat. Neatness is not limited to a clean room; it also includes binders, notes, and school papers. Parents can help lead their teen to mastery by setting consistent expectations. Training a teenager is not always easy, so parents need to set expectations in a way that is not overly critical and allows for their student to make mistakes on her way toward independence.

The biggest visual-spatial challenge for many teenagers is cleaning their room. Like most visual-spatial tasks, cleaning the room can be divided into chunks. First, there are things that belong in the room (eg, school books, bedding, clothes, personal mementos) and those that do not (eg, food, toiletries, trash, dishes). Second, items within a room should have a place. These can be labeled or listed out for teenagers who do not seem to catch on to the order. Start with the most obvious items (clothes in closet, bedding on bed, and school supplies on desk). If your student has problems with understanding the basic visual organization of her room, use blue painter tape to mark out zones in her room. Leave clear pathways from the door to the closet, desk, and bed. Then designate the remaining space to contain messes; for instance, zone A could be for games and activities, zone B could be for clothes, and zone C could be for school projects. This rudimentary system is good for a teenager with delayed organizational skills. Third, you can help your teen through the cleaning process by listing out the cleaning steps (eg, "1. Pick up clothes," "2. Make bed," "3. Remove items that do not belong in the room," "4. Clean desk," and "5. Throw out trash"). For teens who lack spatial organization, they can rely on their sequential processing to turn a visual task into steps.

If your teenager struggles with organizing schoolwork, teach your teen that she can apply the same type of order to her schoolwork that was just described for cleaning her room. Help her set up systems for recording and tracking homework. Encourage her to set up tabs in her binder to delineate subjects and on a weekly basis to make sure that papers end up in the correct spot.

Students that need help with note-taking can be taught strategies to organize visual information, such as mind mapping and other visual formats. These skills allow a student to move away from traditional linear note-taking and allow them to visually see how topics relate (see Appendix C, Mind Mapping).

Athletes rely on instant visual planning.

Athletics provide an example of how important it is to have rapid access to instantaneous mental blueprints. When a skilled basketball player dribbles the ball down the court, for instance, he views the positioning of his teammates and opponents; he may even notice how they are moving, which way their heads are facing, and where they are looking. At once, this visual image triggers a visual blueprint, or plan, for what he will do next. Multiple studies of the cognitive abilities of elite-level athletes have shown that they have superior pattern recognition skills.[32-34] Master chess players, hockey players, basketball players, and football players all share this advantage. Not every teen will be an elite-level athlete, but it is clear that there are advantages for everyone to be able to rapidly create mental blueprints. Math, spelling, note-taking, and reading all improve with rapid visual recall. Parents, teachers, and coaches can promote rapid pattern recognition. Practice will help teens improve their skills, but more important than rehearsing one task thousands of times is to practice many different visual planning activities. Interestingly, elite-level athletes who grew up playing many sports tend to do better at pattern recognition tasks than those who played just one sport from a very young age.[35]

✅ Spatial Organization Recommendations for Teens

Giving Everything a Place

■ A younger teen may need help organizing his or her important materials. Help your teen establish set locations for items such as school supplies, textbooks, car keys, electronics, and shoes. Your teenager should be encouraged to keep his or her possessions in the same designated place every day.

■ Parents can encourage organization in their teen's room by labeling items. There could be labels on shelves and drawers. Clear storage bins could provide visual cues to remind their teen where to store hobbies, projects, and books.

■ Students can use color-coded folders and notebooks to help organize assignments for different academic subjects.

School Organization

■ While it may seem risky to give a student who lacks organization a handheld computer, it can also be liberating for the student to keep all his information (eg, books, notes, and calendar) in one place.

■ Have your teens both keep track of graded assignments and use online grading reports to ensure their record of classwork and exams are up-to-date. Teach them to discuss any discrepancies with their teacher in a timely manner.

Spatial Awareness

■ Older children and teens can improve their spatial awareness by learning and teaching directionality; for example,

- A student could explain how to get from one place to another in school or draw a map.

- An athlete could diagram plays for a team sport.

- A dancer or cheerleader could choreograph a routine.

- While your teens are learning to drive, don't provide every directional step to familiar destinations. Allow the drivers in training the opportunity to be challenged with the decision about which way to turn or what roads to take, to encourage their internalization of the street layout in your town.

Step 4: Practice forward thinking

Your teenager is most likely brilliant and foolish at the same time. There are probably times when you are amazed at your teen's knowledge and are baffled by his inflexibility, shortsightedness, or lack of common sense. As I previously pointed out, the frontal lobe (the part of the brain involved in planning, insight, and big picture thinking) is the last part of the brain to develop; therefore, while your teen may know many things, he very likely continues to make seemingly impulsive and careless mistakes. Even when your teen turns 18, your parenting job is not over. You will need to continue to consistently reinforce many of the lessons that have been in place since your teen was a toddler.

Your teen's planning skills are still underdeveloped. Up until now, he likely has focused on immediate benefits and shown limited interest in the long-term consequences of his behavior. When he left his dish in the sink, you probably cleaned it up; when he forgot his lunch, you probably brought it to school; and when he wasn't studying for a test, you may have reminded him to study. But when it comes time for your student to head off to college, his safety net will be gone. To get your teen ready for college—with the ability to not just get there but stay there—I encourage you to not just teach forward thinking but apply thinking ahead to the specific life skills he will need to survive after he leaves home.

Big Picture Thinking

Teens want freedom and independence, and it is the job of a parent to give those things to a teen, but only when the teen is ready. Successful mastery of life skills is a way for them to demonstrate that they are planning and thinking ahead on a mature level. I suggest pointing out to teens, when they ask for increased freedom, such as staying out late or driving a car, that a good way to show you they are ready for these added responsibilities is by demonstrating that they can make good choices about what I refer to as the 4 Hs: hygiene, health, homework, and household chores and other tasks. They may not automatically make this connection between the 4 Hs and freedom on their own because teens think linearly: "The last time I went out, I came home on time." Whereas, adults think more broadly: "If I cannot count on you to put the milk away after getting cereal, there is no way I can trust you driving a car." So, sharing your criteria for the demonstration of maturity will help them see a broader perspective and use their forming forward-thinking skills to plan accordingly.

Hygiene

Self-care and hygiene is an important indicator of maturity. There is something magical that happens to most teens; at some point, they realize that their odor stinks, and this realization is often triggered by an attraction to a peer. They recognize, for example, that if they look like a slob with uncombed hair, acne, and a smelly body, their peers will be less interested in being close to them. So, by combing his hair and cleaning his body, your teen may actually be forward thinking.

For a while, parents will need to set the expectation for their hygienically disorganized teen. In doing so, they should point out the connection among wearing deodorant and taking showers to prevent body odor, washing one's face and having a clear complexion, and brushing one's teeth to prevent cavities. Be patient with the process. Try not to be judgmental (eg, don't say, "You are gross and you smell bad"), as doing so may alienate your teen. Reinforce the message that taking care of one's body is just part of growing up.

Health

Taking care of one's health includes getting proper amounts of exercise, sleep, and nutrition. Teenagers have a difficult time demonstrating self-control when it comes to their health, and progress in this domain is a sign of maturity.

A growing body of medical research has shown the benefits of sleep on attention, thinking, and health. Research shows that teenagers who get inadequate sleep will perform poorly on academic tests, will more frequently become ill, and will get injured more often when playing sports. A recent study even pointed out that student-athletes who get less than 8 hours of sleep per night are injured more than twice as often as those who are well rested.[35] While those issues are critical to teens' success, as parents we also know that when they do not get enough sleep, they act even more emotionally. Going to bed on time shows the maturity to recognize the body and brain's need for sleep and the ability to execute the planning necessary to make a reasonable bedtime happen. Teenagers need between 8 hours and 11 hours of sleep per night to allow the brain the time it needs to perform its nightly cleansing.

I am fully aware that the demands from homework and after-school activities make 8 or more hours of sleep a difficult goal for some to obtain. Therefore, when a teenager is able to balance activities with the goal of getting enough sleep to perform effectively the next day, he is showing growth in maturity and forward-thinking skills. Teens who demonstrate less maturity will still need support, possibly in the form of having some schedule limitations set. You may want to help your teen get to bed earlier by setting limits on screen time. I recommend keeping electronics out of the bedroom, because not many students, or adults for that matter, show enough self-discipline to turn them off and go to sleep on time.

An organized teen is capable of making healthy food choices. Nutritional foods help a student's school and extracurricular performances. A bowl of cereal for dinner is not a sign of forward thinking, but a meal that includes vegetables and protein is a good way to build brainpower and muscle. A teen not only should learn to make healthy choices but should be able to prepare something nutritious for any of the day's meals and to create some healthy snacks. You can help scaffold this task for your teen by generating a list of healthy meals and snacks that he can prepare for himself. This aid will decrease the frequency with which he opens the pantry and grabs the first item that looks inviting.

Exercise is another way to demonstrate maturity by taking care of one's health. Research clearly demonstrates that people who exercise regularly as children and teens will exercise more as adults. Therefore, things that a parent can do to establish the ethic of fitness in their teen has long-term health benefits. Your teen may not be thinking about adulthood, but he will likely recognize that there are benefits to being in shape: feeling good, looking good, performing better at sports, and improved attention, to name a few. Any teens who act on this awareness and make an effort to improve their mental and physical health tomorrow, by exercising today, are demonstrating forward thinking.

Homework

Managing homework is a complicated task. It requires vigilance to record daily expectations, persistence and stamina to trudge through assignments over the course of an entire school year, and planning to map out and complete long-term assignments. School is not just about learning math, science, and English. Learning the organization and independence needed to manage schoolwork is quite possibly even more important for later life than the subjects themselves.

When your student attended elementary school and middle school, you prepared your child for the demands of school by creating homework routines. You set expectations that homework should not be completed in front of a television set or while instant messaging with friends. If you have not instilled these homework values in your child, it is never too late, but, like all parenting efforts, it becomes more difficult the later you start. If your child has established effective homework strategies, it is likely time for you to pull back your level of support. Remember, during high school, if your teen is ready, you become a consultant, available if called on. An organized teen will work independently and request help from parents as needed. Some teens will require regular check-ins from their parents, but it is a realistic expectation for most teens to independently manage their homework.

Some parents may also not be ready to pull back, even though it is in the best interest of their young learner. In this case, I suggest giving your teen an explanation of your uncertainty. Tell him that you are very proud of him, but raising a teen is a lot of work and that labor of love is a bit traumatizing to a parent. So when it is time to let go, it is difficult. Assuming it is true, tell your teen that you can back off, but you need some reassurance. If your teen can find a way to show you that he is managing his homework routine, that knowledge will help you pull back. For instance, perhaps your 8th grade student could tell you his homework plan each afternoon before going off to his room to get started, or your 9th grader could place his completed homework onto the kitchen table to show it is complete, or maybe your 10th grader could meet with you once a month to review his online grades. Whatever system you agree on, remember that this process of parenting is about your teen growing up as much as it is about you learning to let go.

Household Chores and Other Tasks

Teens can become increasingly independent with their responsibilities, which may include cleaning up after themselves, completing chores, and, for older teens, jobs. Performing these tasks independently shows remarkable growth in maturity. However, realistically, many teens do not master these skills until they move out of the house and realize that they do not like to keep their own space messy and they look forward to their Friday paycheck. Nevertheless, parents should not give up on training these skills, as most tasks demand self-awareness, time management, planning, and follow-through; therefore, as a parent you need to provide the opportunity for your teens to practice and demonstrate forward thinking.

What is the purpose of chores? Chores serve 3 purposes that relate to developing an organized child or teen. First, chores help the entire family. Second, chores teach teens that life requires hard work, and it requires doing things that are sometimes not fun. Third, chores require time management and planning. Helping the family is important for teens who are beginning to realize that the family works better when they help to contribute; the house is neater and Mom and Dad are less stressed. As shown in the Step 5: Promote problem-solving section later in this chapter, chores are one of the ways to encourage better perspective taking from teens. Time management training through chores works when parents are consistent. When I was growing up, my neighbor's mother provided a good model of consistent parenting. I remember sitting in my middle school classroom and hearing my friend's name being called over the intercom so that he would come to the office. When I saw him later that day, he told me that he had forgotten to take the trash out, so his mother called him at school, made him walk the mile home to take out the trash, and walk the mile back carrying a note that said "Feel free to give my son detention for any unexcused classes that he missed today." Instead of punishing her son, my neighbor forced him to deal with the natural consequences of his mistakes. That was the last time my friend forgot to take out the trash.

Having met with thousands of families, I can report that there is tremendous variability among the amount of chores given to teens, and in my opinion, there should be. After all, there are many factors to consider, such as how busy your teen may be. While homework, football, band practice, and student government do not excuse a teen from chores, it is reasonable to acknowledge that if your teen is working hard in other domains that he has learned to put forth effort. So, the purpose of chores for this teen is simply to contribute to the family by cleaning up after himself, making his bed, emptying the dishwasher, cleaning the bathrooms, or doing an hour of yard work on the weekend, which may be enough. On the other hand, if your student coasts through school and does not participate in many activities, it may be a valuable lesson to fill up some of his free time with help around the house and maybe even have him get a job. Teens are getting closer to independence, so they are capable of completing most household chores. Pick chores that are meaningful to the family (not just tasks to keep them busy) so that you can complement them on how they contribute to the family.

At the very minimum, teens should be able to clean up after themselves. Continue to consistently reinforce this message. To avoid confrontation caused by frequent check-ins, make notes of the messes they leave behind and periodically throughout the day, give them the list, and have them clean up. Regarding their room, respect their autonomy by allowing them some freedom about how their room is kept, but provide some consistent standards (eg, "No food in the room," "Dirty clothes should be in the hamper and off the floor").

Allowance continues to be a useful tool for teens. As mentioned before, money encourages planning and forward thinking. However, be careful not to train your teens to think that they should get paid for helping. Reinforce that there are certain things you expect, simply because they live in the house (eg, cleaning up after themselves and making their own bed) and then assign other responsibilities (eg, washing a car, raking leaves) for which you are willing to pay them, because they are being very helpful. Responsible management of money is another sign of developing forward-thinking skills.

Many teens are able to handle a job, and as long as your teen is managing his other responsibilities, a job can be encouraged. The entire experience can be valuable. Seeking a job opening, drafting a resume, and participating in an interview all require elements of planning. Balancing work and other responsibilities offers a great deal of forward-thinking practice. My first job was working at a health club. Once I had some experience, I was given the opportunity to open the club on the morning shift by myself. The night before, my manager showed me the list of responsibilities. I read them over and thought I could handle it, but when I showed up the next morning, I realized that I had no idea how to make coffee and no instructions were on the pot. I should have recognized this the night before, but because I didn't, I had to call my dad for a consultation at 5:00 in the morning—a lesson learned.

In my office, some of my patients' parents frequently express concerns about their teen's use of screen time, because many students are preoccupied with playing games and watching media. Parents are concerned that this obsession interferes with life, and it becomes a major source of conflict. The advice I give to my patients is that I never hear parents express concern about screen time when their kids are mastering the 4 Hs: hygiene, health, homework, and household chores and other tasks. Instead of criticizing kids for their screen time, parents can focus the discussion on what the teen needs to do and not what he wants to do.

Planning Life

Remind your teenager that there is more to life than school. It is important for teens to practice being social, because socialization offers many opportunities for planning. Extracurricular activities such as student government, theater, or sports usually require preparation and should be encouraged. However, face-to-face socialization is also important. Teenagers hanging out together learn to navigate the social world. They make plans together and they help each other deal with boredom. Multiplayer computer gaming is not the same as face-to-face time.

Help your teenagers see that there are opportunities to think ahead during most interactions. They can make predictions about what will be on a test or what a boyfriend might like to do during the weekend. Give your teen the opportunity to plan. A good exercise is to put the teen in charge of 1 dinner per week. Success will require the creation of a shopping list given to a parent before a shopping day and then preparation of the meal in time for dinner. Encourage your teen to make plans with friends so that he can practice forward thinking.

Some teenagers have already figured out their career paths, but if your teen is like most teenagers, he may only know that he wants to attend college and have a vague idea about what to study. The advice I give to parents is that the most important thing at this age is for your teen to have a plan. That goal could be to study engineering at a university, or it could be to attend a junior college for 2 years and then transfer to a 4-year college. The objective could even be to take a year off and backpack throughout Europe. Any of these goals could realistically happen with a plan. Remember that there is a difference between a plan and a goal. If your teen wants to go to Europe, he should know how he is going to get there, where he will sleep, and how he will pay for it; have a safety plan; and more. Likewise, if he is going to college, he must decide what will he study, choose where will he live, and determine how much effort will he put forward toward expenses. The plan is a major component to most successes. When your teen achieves this level of independence, you as a parent will take pride in all the lessons that you have provided for your teen.

 Recommendations for Forward Thinking in Teenagers

Managing Life

- Explain to your teenager that if he demonstrates responsibility in many ways, he has earned the right to increasing freedom. A tangible starting point is to master the 4 Hs: hygiene, health, homework, and household chores and other tasks. Early in your teen's teen years, set standards for the 4 Hs and watch how he performs.

- Expect regular amounts of sleep. If your student has a difficult time meeting his sleep needs, support him by limiting access to electronics as bedtime approaches. Parents should model the behavior that they expect from their teens.

- Teach your teenager to make nutritious meal options so that he can demonstrate healthy choices.

- Encourage your teen to get regular exercise by pointing out the short- and long-term benefits of being in better physical condition.

- Many teenagers are ready to manage their homework independently. At this point, the role of the parent is to become a consultant. If your teen is not ready for this level of independence, meet your teen at his level, but help him work toward homework independence.

- Assign chores to your student that are of value to the family, not just work to keep him busy. Base the amount of chores that you give on how much nonschool-related time he has available. Students with less activities and homework can be given more chores to help them appreciate that hard work is needed no matter what path in life they chose to take.

- Consistently reinforce the message that your teen should clean up after himself. Try making lists of things he leaves behind as a periodic and gentle reminder for him to clean up.

- Money management is a good way to practice planning. Allowance can be earned, and encourage your teen to save for things that he wants to purchase.

- If your teen is managing his health, hygiene, homework, and household chores and other tasks, he may be ready for a job. Seeking and keeping a job challenges forward-thinking skills.

Predicting and Planning Life

- Older students should be encouraged to predict what a teacher will have on a test. Teachers can encourage students to write down these predictions to get a better understanding if the teacher grasps what is most important to a topic.

- Give your teen real-life planning practice. For example, have your teen plan one of the days of your family's next vacation. Make sure he considers not only what to do but the time it will take, transportation, expenses, and how to be prepared for the event, such as what to wear and what to bring.

Step 5: Promote problem-solving

Problem-solving is the most complex aspect of organized thinking because it pushes simultaneous processing (the brain's ability to entertain multiple thoughts at the same time) to the limits. During the teenage years, there is a tremendous capacity for growth in problem-solving skills, and it is the job of parents to nurture this development. A teenager who gets the big picture can be responsible, creative, productive, and generous. The most organized thinkers are respected by others and generally become leaders.

Remember, however, that development happens along a continuum; therefore, do not get too excited that your early-to-develop teen is on the cusp of greatness, or become too disappointed that your late-to-blossom teen is not yet showing insight. Her prefrontal cortex, the part of the brain responsible for the executive functions (the ability to plan, organize, initiate, and problem-solve), continues to develop until her late 20s.

A patient's mother explained to me that her daughter always seems to have a small crisis before a big event such as a trip, family party, school test, or competition. What happens is that before one of these events, the parent will ask her to do a few basic chores. Her daughter will say that she cannot, because she has too much work to do. When her parents remind her that reasoning doesn't work, she does the chore but then is angry at her parents for hours. This is a repeated struggle, and it seems that she should be able to recognize the solution, but despite parental coaching, she hasn't yet figured out that she creates the situation by procrastinating on homework. She waits to write her papers, leaves belongings scattered in her room, and doesn't start studying until she absolutely needs to. In her mind, she is leaving herself time, but she does not recognize that sometimes other people will also have expectations for her that will take time; therefore, she leaves herself no buffer. Had she kept her room neat or started her work earlier, requests from her parent would be less of a frustration. This sort of egocentrism is common among teenagers. Continual teaching about perspective taking and problem-solving is important.

Your teenager's abilities in most areas (eg, topic knowledge) will exceed her organized thinking skills, and your teen will probably not have a complete grasp of the big picture—and that is OK. This section focuses on the lessons you can teach your teen during the teen years to help her develop the problem-solving skills that she will need as a young adult.

Perspective Taking

Because teens have difficulty taking perspective, young teens are often egocentric. Their short-sightedness is a large part of what makes parenting a teen so difficult. The rules and boundaries that a parent puts into place may not make sense from a teen's perspective. The teen might think, "Why should I clean my room? It is my room," or "Why do I need to clean the kitchen, when I never made the mess?" However, by the time your teen heads off to college, he will start to have a broader view of the world. Your older teen may become an activist as he tries to conquer life's inequalities. Your older teen may gradually begin to show some interest in his younger siblings. Being able to take perspective will be important as your teen heads out into the world where he will encounter many different people with conflicting viewpoints to his own. Prepare your teen for this transition by exposing him to new situations and the plights of others. Be kind, help others, and encourage community service so that he can get an appreciation of, for instance, the struggles of people who face homelessness, the experiences of elderly people, or barriers for minorities or people with disabilities.

Learning about people's differences may help your teenager recognize his own strengths and weaknesses. Self-awareness is another important milestone for a teenager. A teen who is self-aware is in a position to strategically improve on a weakness. He may figure out that he needs to study differently for a test or rehearse with a partner for an audition to the school play. Until your teen becomes self-aware, he may find it difficult to take feedback and so act defensively. Another big advantage of self-awareness is that now your teen may realize when he needs help. Most teens struggle at some point during high school or college, whether it be academically, socially, or emotionally. Those who are able to ask for help have more tools to deal with their struggles. Model humility for your teen. Your teen will know more than you do about certain things, so ask him for help. My children are talented with electronics and so I frequently consult with them when my phone freezes or my computer won't let me save my work. Asking your teenagers for help will help build their self-confidence and help them understand that it is OK to ask for help.

Creative Planning and Imaginative Thinking

Friends should get together and invent, write, and create. Support your teen's efforts to get together with friends and make them turn off the electronics. Look for ways to encourage imagination. Teens are often motivated by money. Help your teen think about creative ways to make money. Each year, my kids make peppermint bark, which they sell at the local craft fair. They love the experience and their business has been so successful that they have orders each year from retuning customers.

A new trend in high school is to ask friends out on a date in a creative way. I love this idea, as it encourages imagination, but it also, I think, decreases the likelihood of rejection. After all, who is going to say no to a student who goes through the effort of filling a perspective date's bedroom with balloons and has a sign that reads, "Don't burst my bubble—go to the dance with me!"?

Problem-solving

Your student should be able to formulate and execute a plan. To acquire this skill, you must allow him to do things for himself. Encourage him to choose his own class schedule, make plans for the weekend, figure out his transportation to the movies, and solve his own boredom with activities other than video games. It is perfectly acceptable for your teenager to consult with you about these problems, but most important, you want to convey the confidence that he can solve them himself.

One strategy I use to help my patients solve problems is to teach them about *relevance* and *importance.* These 2 criteria can be used to help your teen learn to prioritize. For instance, if he is pulling weeds or doing homework and he receives a text message, it is very unlikely that the text is *relevant* to the task at hand. On the other hand, if he is searching the Internet for a summer internship at a tech company and he sees an article about the newest product from that company, there is some relevance, and a brief diversion may be acceptable. Encourage your teen to determine whether something is relevant by modeling appropriate behavior. For instance, unless you are a physician who takes emergency phone calls, you most likely do not need to answer or look at your phone during a family dinner. The other measuring stick is *importance.* When studying or preparing for a test, very few activities are as important as the acts of studying and sleeping. Once again, responding to a text message, answering the phone, or getting a snack should be a lesser priority. Of course, if the task is to make plans for the weekend, answering a text message is both relevant and important.

The Big Picture

The ability to grasp the big picture is what many consider to be the pinnacle of organized thinking. Big picture thinkers are able to consider multiple alternatives (simultaneously) and to recognize the essential details in any given situation. They can listen to a teacher lecture and know what is going to be on a test. They can recognize when someone is unhappy and know how to make her feel better. They can provide a concise summary of a movie or a book that they read. They prioritize. They solve problems. They don't stress over little things, and they don't waste time on unnecessary tasks. They don't get bogged down by black-and-white thinking; instead, they are able to think flexibly when making decisions. People respect their opinions, and they can easily grow into leaders.

The concept of importance is at the heart of understanding the big picture. Enlightened teenagers have a sense of what is important. A good example is school spirit. It is fun to get caught up in the excitement of cheering for one's school in a sporting match. But some teens get too caught up in the excitement and lose perspective. Sometimes they taunt an opposing player or yell at a fan from the other team. I have seen parents also lose their sense of reality at sport settings and scream at officials. The big picture is that school sports are a great way for kids to stay healthy, learn teamwork, and strive for excellence, and an enlightened coach and his teen players and fans demonstrate the big picture by exhibiting good sportsmanship.

One of my favorite "getting a grasp of the big picture" memories was when I watched my tween-aged son, who, without specifically being instructed to do so, made sure that a basketball teammate who had autism felt included as a part of the team during his limited time on the court. This player had minimal athletic ability and skills, but he loved being on the team. The coach, who had a wonderful sense of the big picture, always made sure that the child received playing time, no matter how close the score. And my son, who was the point guard, always found a way to get this student the ball, even if it meant passing up an easy shot. The team recognized that it was more important for everyone on the team to feel valued than to run up the score in a random middle school basketball game.

It is exciting to watch your teen's insight grow. As he moves through his teen years, he will comprehend books, political issues, and perspectives with increasing depth. Encourage dinner table discussions about important issues. Instead of trying to convince your teenager to agree with your opinion, play devil's advocate and challenge him to think about both sides of an issue. An insightful student makes good choices. He realizes that getting enough sleep is critical to his academic success and physical health, he knows that in order to do well on a test he must study, and he realizes that he can help out his family by doing some chores.

The teen years should be fun, but they should also provide a student with the experiences he will need to decide what he wants to do after high school and college. The students that are most prepared to make these decisions are the ones who have explored many options during their teen years. That is why I recommend to my patients and my own children that after age 12, teenagers should try 1 or 2 new things each year: join a club, play on a team, volunteer, play chess, collect coins, or mow lawns, for example. It doesn't really matter what they do, but each experience, good or bad, should help point them in a direction. If they volunteer at a preschool and decide that they do not like young children or if they get a job landscaping and learn that they like to work with their hands, they have either "ruled in" or ruled out some possibilities. Each new experience will help your teen think about the big picture goal of figuring out what he wants to do with his life.

By the time your student finishes high school, the big picture is that he needs to have a future plan. He may not have yet selected a career, but the plan should include steps toward figuring out his future. And whatever plan he chooses may, of course, change. For some, starting work after high school is expected. For others, a 2-year junior college is best, many are ready for a 4-year university, and others may take a gap year to travel or work. Whatever direction your teen selects, he needs to think though the next steps. If he does want to take a nontraditional path, such as traveling, be sure to emphasize the importance of designing and organizing his conceptualized trip. As mentioned earlier, deciding to backpack through Europe is not specific enough; that is a goal, not a plan. He must determine how he will pay for the trip and manage all associated travel logistics.

With increasing age comes increasing demands, and your teen will need to make increasingly important decisions, including choosing what to study, calculating safe driving maneuvers, deciding where to work, and deciding who to choose to date. Since nobody leaving home for the first time is completely ready to be self-sufficient, your teen also needs to know how to ask for help. To perform both problem-solving and self-advocacy, he needs to know how to solve problems.

Recommendations to Promote Problem-solving With Teenagers

Exploring

■ It is important for teens to try new things. The more experiences that they have, the easier it will be for them to someday select a career path. Encourage your teen to try at least one new activity every year.

■ With the appropriate supervision, teens should have time to hang out with their friends. It is during this free time when they can challenge their imagination.

Problem-solving

■ Empower your teens the opportunity to make plans by letting them plan for themselves. Prompt your teen with questions (eg, "How will you get there?" "How much will it cost?" "Who will be there?" "How will you get home?") in order to make the plans more complete.

■ You can model problem-solving for your child or teen by sharing your current issues and demonstrating how you deal with them or by recalling past dilemmas and how things were handled. Show them how you think through your predicaments.

■ When teens come to you with a problem, do not immediately work to solve it for them. Let them struggle a bit. Suggest brainstorming activities to help them consider the possibilities. Once they have a list of options, help them determine criteria for making a decision. But, ultimately, let them make a plan for how to tackle the situation.

■ During the teenage years, your student should become increasingly independent, managing her own calendar. Consider using a shared calendar tool so that you can easily communicate family events.

■ Teens should be responsible for their own schoolwork, tracking grades and managing relationships with their teachers, advisors, and coaches.

■ Encourage your teens to make plans for the summer. Help them think about chores, jobs, study time (if any), and adventures. Let your teen set summer goals and then create plans to reach his objective.

- Have your teens take the lead on obtaining their driver's permit and license. Help them plan the steps and make the appointments for training and testing.

- Allow older teens to take responsibility for their future. Give them direction, but let them find their own jobs. Offer support, but let them manage their college applications, completing forms and preparing for entrance exams.

- Whether he is taking a gap year or going to college, make sure that your teen has a plan by the time he finishes high school.

- Help your teenagers learn to prioritize by using relevance and importance as guiding principles. Build their big picture thinking capabilities by practicing skills such as summarization, making inferences, being flexible, and using creative problem-solving.

Perspective Taking

- Community service can enrich your teen's perspective and help him better understand the thoughts of others.

- Listen to your teens' perspectives as they describe the peer drama at school, and encourage them to think about why their friends behave that way.

Chapter 8

Organized Children Are Raised

Organized children do not just suddenly appear—*they are raised*. And now, parents, you have the power to guide your children to use organized thinking. In *Raising an Organized Child,* you have read about developmentally appropriate organizational expectations that require critical neurodevelopmental abilities including sequential and spatial thinking, memory, and working memory (the ability to process more than one thing at a time). These abilities in children grow when properly supported and allow your children to track their possessions, clean up after themselves, organize their thoughts, and anticipate and plan.

I emphasize development in this book because children are constantly growing and changing. As they progress, we as parents need to raise the bar and push them gently to the next level. When they are ready to pick out their own clothes, pack their own lunch, walk to a neighbor's house, or ride their bike to school, let them, and encourage them along the way. The intellectual challenge stimulates brain growth, and the feeling of accomplishment promotes self-esteem. Yet we must keep realistic expectations. Pushing children too soon or too hard leads to frustration. This book guides parents to a better understanding of their child's organizational strengths and weaknesses, which should make it easier to encourage growth and set appropriate expectations.

Parents, remember to be patient. Some children will bloom early and others much later. The part of the brain that supports organization often continues to develop until an individual's late 20s. Support your child's progress, and do not make struggling too stressful by pointing out every mistake. Research has shown that positive parenting works: tell 4-year-olds or 14-year-olds that they are hard workers and that you are proud of them and watch them smile and light up with pride. We have 18 years to get them ready for college and adulthood. Do not worry if your 5-year-old has not mastered cleaning up his toys, if your 10-year-old forgets to write down homework assignments, or if your 15-year-old still forgets to do his daily chores. Be patient, be consistent, and keep encouraging your child or adolescent for success. As parents, our job along the way is to arm them with valuable lessons and the neurodevelopmental abilities to grow into hardworking, well-adjusted, and kind adults.

My wife and I have learned important parenting lessons along the way that help us manage the stress of parenting 5 children. First, please know, **you are not alone.** My parents dealt with my missteps when I was growing up, and my friends, most of which are excellent parents, question their own parenting skills from time to time. All parents struggle. Thousands of families have sought out my professional help. Being a parent is not easy; there is no instruction manual that comes with your new baby's arrival. Yet the steps outlined in this book can help guide parents to build their child's organizational skills throughout their childhood. You will find yourself referring back to this book as your baby turns into a toddler, and your toddler turns into a child, and before you know it, your baby will be a teenager. As your child grows, you can turn the page to the next chapter and adjust your parenting guidance.

Organizational training begins at birth and continues into young adulthood. Starting during their children's infancy, parents can encourage growth in their children's organizational skills. They can establish a learning environment through consistency. We consistently help meet the needs of our children, thereby preventing toxic stress and laying the foundation for the first sequences. By us being consistent, children learn that there is organization in the world around them. They are comforted by their routines, feeding schedule, and special bedtime rituals. After 8 months of age, most infants are beginning to learn sequencing on their own through cause and effect. So proactive parents can encourage this growth with appropriate toys and by playing 2-step games such as peekaboo.

Toddlers are amazing. The transformation from an infant to a walking, talking, being silly, and playful toddler is miraculous. They are little sponges exploring the world and learning. Research shows that dramatic brain growth happens during the toddler years. This period marks a tremendous opportunity for parents to support their child's organizational skills. The toddler years are a time to share sequences with your child. Continue to use consistent daily routines and to introduce order by using temporal words such as *after, during,* and *before.* Count, sing, and tell nursery rhymes, all of which have an inherent order. Demonstrate for your toddler that tasks have a beginning, a middle, and an end, and have fun playing games during which you learn to take turns. You can also reinforce spatial awareness by ensuring that everything has a place. Create an organized environment so that your child can understand, visualize, and remember where things can be found. Play with puzzles and balls to promote the development of your child's visual processing (the ability to make sense of the information taken in through the eyes). Even though your child is still very young, she will begin to show signs of forward thinking. Celebrate your toddler's creativity and humor. Avoid doing everything for your child. Let your child struggle a little bit while she tries to figure things out for herself. And be sure to record home movies of everything along the way because this wonderful time passes by too quickly.

The foundation set by consistent parenting of your infant and toddler begins to pay off during the preschool years. Early established routines, such as bedtime and feeding, lead to increased compliance by young children.

Language explodes during the preschool years. During these years, your child will learn tens of thousands of new words. Support your child's language development by reading books and telling stories. Talk with your child. The progress that your child makes in language will greatly increase his opportunities for learning. At this age, and with new language skills, your child will be able to understand concepts. Words can be used to teach order, spatial awareness, and forward thinking. Directional terms such as *over, under, near, beneath,* and *between* build a conceptual understanding of visual-spatial relationships for your child. And if you share your plans and schedules, your child will see how forward thinking occurs. Despite these newly formed skills, the preschool years can be the first of many challenging years for parents because preschoolers begin to assert their independence—the so-called terrible twos. Try not to worry about your child's meltdowns. They are signs of frustration and go away more quickly when parents remain calm and maintain their consistent routines. Remember to teach your child to be patient and to solve problems on his own, because this will help reduce his frustrations. And one of the greatest opportunities for your preschooler to learn is through his imagination. So take time to be silly, role-play, create imagination, and build things with your child, so that he has the necessary skills for the school years.

School age is a period during which there is massive growth in skill acquisition. During this time, school-aged children learn to read and tell time, and by middle school, many children independently manage their own homework. A school-aged child learns "step wisdom" and becomes a master of routines, and your job is to teach these routines so that your child can increasingly function independently. A young child can learn basic routines such as toileting and dressing, while an older child can effectively manage time and materials. Your child will gain confidence through competence and earn independence by demonstrating responsibility.

Do more than just teach routines; show your child how to break tasks down into steps so that he will be prepared to overcome new obstacles on his own.

Always remember that your child is learning and will likely make many mistakes along the way. You can help your child make better choices by consistently setting clear expectations. When your child makes a mistake or breaks a rule, apply natural consequences to reinforce the cause and effect relationship between actions and consequences. Punishment is usually not necessary when natural consequences are appropriately applied. If you find yourself feeling the need to frequently punish your child, consult your pediatrician to see if your child needs special help or if perhaps you could learn new parenting strategies. It is very likely that your school-aged child's behavior will seem sloppy and careless at times. A good skill to reinforce during this age is to be a "closer." Encourage your child to finish what he starts and finish in a way in which he is most proud of the outcome.

Children are egocentric during their preschool years, but during middle school, they begin to take perspective and become more likely to grasp the big picture and "the greater good." To build insight and logic, have your child think deeply. When she says things that do not make sense, challenge her to explain herself. Ask her to make predictions, to estimate outcomes, and to solve problems. Do not let your child get sucked into passive activities such as social media and video games. Challenge your school-aged child to be creative and imaginative.

As your child grows, your role as a parent should also evolve. During the school-age years, your role will change from being a coach to a manager, and during the teen years, you become more like a consultant. Teenagers want, and really need, to experience independence. However, letting go can be tricky because your teen's priorities may be different from your own. And, your teen's swirling hormones may make her emotions erratic, making you question her maturity. Keep being steady for your teen. Listen and show acceptance. Enforce consistent and appropriate boundaries, and respond calmly. Help your teen understand that what you require to feel more confident about her independence is for her to manage her needs too. A teen who takes care of her health, hygiene, homework, and household chores and other tasks, and manages to engage in face-to-face social activities, is well on the way toward independence. Whenever realistic, encourage your child or teen to make choices for herself and then learn from both her successes and failures.

From the time that your child is born to beyond the time that he moves out, he will need your support. His executive function (brain skills needed to plan, organize, and complete tasks) will be evolving. The recommendations in this book can be used to guide parents as they gradually help their child become a more organized thinker. Adhere to the 5 Steps to Raising an Organized Child.

1. Be consistent.
2. Introduce order.
3. Give everything a place.
4. Practice forward thinking: planning, estimating, and creativity.
5. Promote problem-solving.

Following these rules, parents and teachers can help children become organized thinkers by strengthening the neuro-circuitry needed to process sequential, spatial, and simultaneous information.

The world is full of problems to be solved, and young students are the problem-solvers of the future. Teaching your children to be organized starting when they are very young and continuing through young adulthood will give them the best opportunity to be prepared for life. Be consistent in how you teach these lessons. Share with your child a sense of time and space so that he understands order. Practice forward thinking by allowing him to plan and anticipate for himself. And encourage an understanding of the big picture by modeling it in your behavior and by promoting perspective taking. Your organized child will someday thank you with his future success.

Appendix A

Misunderstood Minds

Executive dysfunctions (weaknesses in the brain functions that support goal-directed action, self-monitoring, attention, response inhibition, and coordination of complex thought) have been associated with numerous neurological conditions, including, but not limited to, schizophrenia, Alzheimer disease, autism spectrum disorder (ASD), attention-deficit/ hyperactivity disorder (ADHD), fetal alcohol syndrome, post-traumatic stress disorder, and depression. This does not mean that just because someone has executive dysfunctions, she will end up with one of these conditions. Instead, it means that if someone has one of these conditions, she will very likely also have executive dysfunctions. A growing body of medical research demonstrates the frontal lobe changes that occur in people who have these and other conditions, and I would argue that these executive challenges are some of the most disabling aspects for children with these conditions. I have chosen 2 well-studied conditions that affect executive functions in children, ASD and ADHD, to demonstrate how the symptoms of disorganization are at the core of these conditions.

Autism Spectrum Disorder

"I am convinced that my child's future success both academically and socially has everything to do with my son's organization."

—*Maureen, mother of a 15-year-old with autism*

This quote by the mother of one of my patients stemmed from her
15 years of discovery about the mind of her child with ASD. He was
well-behaved, was polite, and, with support, achieved good grades in high
school. Yet, he consistently forgot to perform tasks that are critical for daily
self-care; without prompting from his mother, he would neglect his hygiene
and would even frequently forget to eat lunch.

Autism is considered a spectrum disorder, suggesting that children
with this condition are different but share varying amounts of common
symptoms. While the precise cause of autism is not known, it seems that
multiple factors, including a genetic predisposition, can cause this disorder.
The Centers for Disease Control and Prevention reports that autism, also
known as ASD, exists in 1 out of 59 individuals.[37] This statistic represents
a 15-fold increase in the number of cases compared with 25 years ago.
Characteristics of autism usually appear in the first 3 years after birth.
Children with autism have differences in social communication skills,
which may or may not include delays in the appearance of typical early
language milestones, and a tendency toward restricted and repetitive
behaviors. In addition, their sensory system may be unusually sensitive
or insensitive to noises, textures, tastes, or pain. Children with ASD can
have associated challenges with attention, learning, intelligence, emotional
regulation, and motor coordination. At the core of many of these vulnerabilities is an inability to integrate and synthesize neurological information
from all parts of the brain. Frontal lobe dysfunction has been observed,
and clinical executive dysfunctions are recognized, in children with autism.

There can be a generalized disorganization about the way that children
with autism process information. They can have problems with multilevel
processing, such that too much simultaneous neurological information
makes their brains run less efficiently. A classic example is the lack of eye
contact made by children with autism. It has been hypothesized that if
they divert the amount of mental effort needed to use their eyes to read
body language, their thoughts get mixed up, and so they avoid eye contact

and as a result do not practice this skill. As they get older, eye contact can become more difficult to learn.

Multitasking is also important for perspective taking. The *Theory of Mind* refers to the process of attributing a mental state (eg, a belief, an emotion) to another in order to predict or understand that person's behavior, and how it is affected is believed to be a core feature of autism.[38] For instance, the mother of one of my patients with high-functioning autism related a story about a difficult experience her son had taking a high school algebra test. Her son was a good student with an A average in the class. His father, who studied with the boy the night before the test, reported that he was adequately prepared. However, when the teacher passed out the examination, my patient realized that he did not have a pencil. He sat at his desk for 45 minutes and stared at the test until it was time to turn in his blank paper. When I asked him what else he could have done in that situation, he acknowledged that he did not think to ask for assistance. When I pointed out that requesting help was an option, his response revealed his poor perspective taking, "The teacher would have given me a pencil if she wanted me to have one." Problems with perspective sharing are seen as central to the social and communicative symptoms of children with ASD. Taking the perspective of another requires multilevel processing. Personal assumptions must be put on hold in the working memory (a type of memory responsible for temporarily holding information during mental processing, which allows for the mental manipulation of stored information) while thinking about what another person is thinking. To successfully take perspective, one must simultaneously consider the prior experience of others, interpret the context of the situation for the other person, have an understanding of body language, and use eye contact. The Theory of Mind challenges seen in children with autism may be considered to be at least in part the result of disorganized thinking and demonstrate how social cognition is affected by the executive functions.

A deficit in insight and big picture thinking is a symptom that becomes increasingly obvious as children with autism become tweens and teens. These abilities are referred to as *higher-order thoughts,* because performance of these takes multiple simultaneous thoughts. Big picture thinkers are capable of considering multiple alternatives before coming to a decision that is good not only for them, but for everyone, and this capacity is diminished in children with autism and children with deficits in executive functioning.

Early on in the development of a child with autism, changes in the brain can be detected. Brain growth is abnormally rapid in the dorsal and medial frontal cortex early in life. This finding likely accounts for the large head circumference seen in many children with autism.[37] Under normal brain development, neural network connections are formed, but some are subsequently eliminated through a process known as "pruning." The pruning refines normal brain conditions and increases the efficiency of the remaining connections in the brain. One hypothesis is that the brain of some children who have autism undergoes less pruning. This, in turn, may account for the "traffic jams," a confused neural network that affects social and verbal communication and the ability to accurately process sensory information.

Child developmental and neurological research studies, to look at child development and early brain development, have supported the idea that executive functions are less developed in children with autism. Functional imaging studies (visual representations of blood flow to various parts of the brain while a patient does a specific task, such as math) by Zilbovicius and others[39] and Ozonoff and others[40] provide structural evidence that many of the differences seen in children who have autism originate in the frontal lobe. Three-year-old children who have autism showed low levels of frontal cerebral blood flow, resembling the levels of normal blood flow in 1-year-olds. Behavioral studies tracking executive functions correlate with these findings by providing further evidence of frontal lobe involvement. Other research comparing children with ASD with control groups have demonstrated executive function deficits. Children with autism struggle on the Dimensional Card Sort Task described in the "Following Rules" box of Chapter 1, Child Development and Brain Organization. They do not effectively shift from the color rule to the picture rule. Across multiple studies, people with ASD were found to be deficient in executive functioning skills such as planning, mental flexibility, self-control (control of one's behavioral and emotional impulses), and self-monitoring.[40-42]

The way in which children with autism process language also reflects the disorganization of their brains. Serious language delays in children with autism often predict worse outcomes in independent functioning as adults. Even though language differences are central to autism, many children with autism develop large and, sometimes, advanced vocabularies. They can have encyclopedic knowledge about topics, and many have the ability to recite scripts from movies or television shows they watch. The problem, therefore, is not with word knowledge, but with the ability to communicate, that is, to construct and provide an organized thought in a way that the audience will understand, sometimes referred to as *language pragmatics*. Children with autism can struggle to effectively communicate their needs. One of my clients was kicked off the public bus after an altercation with another rider. My patient rode the public bus to his work program every day and liked to sit up front near the bus driver. One day, another rider was in "his" seat. My client's response was to stand directly in front of the rider. While leaning over the rider in a presumably unintentionally aggressive posture, he proceeded to grunt like a caveman until the rider moved. Despite having functional language skills, my client could not plan an appropriate verbal response. As a result, he was no longer allowed to ride the bus.

The sensory system of children with autism can be highly disorganized. As a physician, I have learned as much from my patients as I have from the books that I have studied. One subject that is underrepresented in the literature, but very real in the lives of many of my patients, is sensory integration (how the brain processes and makes use of information obtained through our various senses). Books did not prepare me for the violent response a child can have to the seam of a sock, the taste of a new food, or the noise of a toilet flushing. Some children, especially many of those with autism, experience exaggerated responses to environmental stimuli. It is as if their bodies cannot modulate the sensory input. When overwhelmed by the environment, the child's already diminished skills become even more impaired. Her brain is overloaded by too much simultaneous information.

My clinical observations about multisensory processing are consistent with the research findings that there is a neurological basis for sensory integration deficits in children who have autism.[24,25,43] Children with autism struggle when they are placed into situations that require them to process multiple pieces of information simultaneously. Their social and communication skills often decline when they are in crowded, noisy, or busy situations. Many parents of my patients with autism avoid birthday parties, movie theaters, and public restrooms (fearing the automatic flushing toilets) because those settings are too difficult for their children to tolerate. Correspondingly, treatment often involves the elimination of unnecessary stimuli and the gradual introduction, or desensitization, to increasing layers of environmental stimulation.

Treatment and Education of Autistic and related Communication handicapped Children (TEACCH) is an intervention approach used in part by most school systems to support children with autism.[44] According to the evidence that children are overwhelmed by too much information, TEACCH classrooms are highly structured with predictable routines displayed on visual lists. In some classrooms, students are placed into a small cubicle or "cubby" to do work, and over time, a side of the cubby is removed, thereby gradually increasing the child's exposures to the environment.

Similarly, sensory integration therapy is designed to assist in the organization and processing of the senses. This therapy does not usually involve the development of specific skills but instead consists of sensory process training, exposing students to various levels of sensory input and eliminating distracting or irritating sensory input. This may increase a child's ability to participate in the world, teaching him to sit in a noisy classroom or tolerate the clothes he wears. Scientific studies regarding the effectiveness of sensory integration therapy are limited and inconclusive, but, nevertheless, it is widely used by families of children with autism and ADHD.

Some parents of children with autism place their children onto specialized diets, the most popular of which is the gluten-free/casein-free diet. Like with sensory integration therapy, research does not at this time support the practice. It is not clear whether specialized diets work in children with autism, or perhaps in a subpopulation of children with autism. There are various theories as to why a specialized diet may help children. The most widely accepted theory supports the concept that disorganized, multilevel processing relates to food susceptibility. In other words, if a child with autism has an allergy or a food sensitivity, this creates a distraction for the child's brain, which can detract from other mental processes. According to this theoretical model, elimination of a food irritant from a child's diet may potentially increase the child's ability to function.

Children with ASD demonstrate repetitive behaviors and speech. Some behaviors such as rocking, pacing, and staring at their fingers have been referred to as *self-stimulatory behaviors*. Children with autism perform these behaviors most frequently when they are anxious or excited, and some seem to relax while performing their repetitive tasks. Some of my high-functioning patients perform repetitive tasks, such as spinning themselves on a swing, to relax after a difficult day at school. The drive for sameness or repetition can, in itself, be disabling when it becomes so persistent that it interferes with spoken communication or participation in activities. It is not clear why children who have autism behave like this. However, following the model of a disorganized mind, children with autism have a busy neural network of "freeways." They cannot efficiently direct their mental traffic, and so a default pathway that feels familiar, comfortable, and safe takes precedence. Like a rut in a road, the more that road is traveled, the deeper the rut becomes, until all traffic drifts into the same repetitive rut. When we treat children with autism, we begin with organization and structure and gradually introduce flexibility and options and exposures to new situations.

Attention-deficit/hyperactivity Disorder

> *"How is it that my child can focus for hours as he takes apart and reassembles the most complicated Lego models, but when we ask him to do homework, he falls apart?"*
>
> —*Mother of a 10-year-old who has attention-deficit/hyperactivity disorder*

This question, from the mother of one of my 10-year-old patients, addresses one of the confounding complexities of the struggles of children with attention deficits. There are circumstances when this child's attention is great, and at other times, this child can struggle to maintain focus. So, one can see why many parents may jump to the conclusion that their child with ADHD is just "lazy." The reality, however, is that attention is a complex system comprised of many attention components (eg, attention span, consistency, effort, self-control) and that breakdowns in just a couple of the domains is more than enough to cause a child to struggle at home and at school. Just like in children who have autism, executive dysfunctions are evident in children with ADHD.

Attention-deficit/hyperactivity disorder, also known as ADHD, is a developmental condition that dramatically affects 4% to 8% of adolescents and adults, as well as young boys and girls.[45,46] Increasingly, we are recognizing that ADHD is not a behavior disorder, but a developmental impairment of some or all of the brain's executive functions. One leading expert in the field of ADHD is Russell A. Barkley, PhD. According to Dr Barkley, the assessment of ADHD impairment is best done by evaluating an individual's performance in the various domains of daily life: how the individual is performing in meeting daily demands, responsibilities, and other academic, social, occupational, or family obligations will be far more sensitive indicators of ADHD than will evaluations of the individual's knowledge about how to do these things.[22,47] Many of the executive dysfunctions described earlier in this book are found in children with ADHD, including difficulties with prioritizing, planning, initiating, and completing tasks in a timely manner; difficulty organizing time; difficulty managing materials; difficulty with behavioral flexibility; a high level of procrastination; forgetfulness; and poor working memory. More and more researchers recognize that ADHD affects not just behavior, but also physical and emotional self-control.

Attention-deficit/hyperactivity disorder is a disorder that affects several brain regions, but mostly it affects the prefrontal cortex (the part of the brain at the very front of the frontal lobe responsible for planning and organized thinking, among other tasks). Brain imaging studies document the biological reality of ADHD. Studies looking at the brain structure suggest that there is a reduction in the volume of the brain in children with ADHD and an overall delay in its development, particularly in the frontal lobe.

Further evidence that executive dysfunctions are at the core of ADHD symptoms is demonstrated by the medications used to treat ADHD for more than 80 years, first reported in 1973 by Charles Bradley. All currently approved medications for ADHD, both stimulants and non-stimulants, work by making the prefrontal cortex, among other areas, work more effectively.[48] Millions of children and adults have taken stimulant medications to treat ADHD. Studies have demonstrated how these medications improve executive functions and normalize behavioral impairments.[49,50] The executive functions of children taking medication showed dramatic improvements.[51] The correlation between improved executive functioning and stimulant medication is so strong that some researchers have proposed that successful treatment with a stimulant medication is confirmation of a diagnosis of ADHD. It has been found that children with ADHD and autism, as well as more than a dozen other conditions, also often have executive dysfunctions. These deficits are often the most frustrating for parents and the most disabling for children. The strategies described in this book are applicable to all children with executive dysfunctions, regardless of the cause or origin. They apply to children with ADHD and autism as much as they do any disorganized child. However, children with these conditions often develop organizational skills more slowly than their peers. Patience and perseverance is important for parents.

Appendix B

Creating Mini Routines

Children who experience disorganized thinking tend to have the most difficulty during unstructured times. One obvious unstructured activity is recess at school when chaotic thinkers wander from one activity to the next, run into conflicts because of unmet expectations, or do not initiate any activity. Disorganized thinkers have experienced frequent lapses in organized thinking that result in seemingly unpredictable periods of unstructured time. For instance, after brushing his teeth, Johnny puts down his toothbrush and leaves the bathroom. Because of his disorganized mind, brushing his teeth did not trigger the next steps in the bathroom sequence (eg, putting away his toothbrush, using the toilet, and washing his face). Even seemingly predictable steps of mini routines, such as brushing teeth, can seem like an unstructured task to a disorganized child. It can help to make plans for these unstructured times, by subdividing these mini routines into *mini* mini routines.

Mini routines need to be individualized to meet the needs of each child and each family. For young children, the routines can be listed as a series of pictures. Below are sample mini routines that can be copied and used. However, I suggest the following techniques when creating your own mini routines:

1. Decide on what mini routines create the most family struggle. Common times when mini routines should be put into place usually occur when everyone in the house is getting ready (eg, for work, for bed, for

school, for dinner) or transitioning (eg, arriving home). But eventually, mini routines can be created for other activities such as homework, playtime, errands, and lazy weekend mornings.

2. Decide what you want each activity to look like. Do you want your child to perform the tasks independently or with help? Do you want the tasks to happen within a time frame?

3. Create mini routines. It is important, whenever possible, to involve a child in creating these lists. This will encourage your child to think about the consideration that goes into being organized.

4. Write the mini routines, but try to limit mini routines to 5 steps. Remember that mini routines can be combined to form larger routines such as getting ready for school. Picture lists are often needed for children who are unable to speak, read, or write.

5. Determine where to keep the lists. It may be useful to post the lists where they will most often be used (eg, on the bathroom mirror, on the refrigerator, by the front door, on the ceiling above a child's bed) or laminated on note cards that are placed onto a ring and carried with the child or the parent.

6. Choose 1 or 2 mini routines at first, and once the tasks have been mastered, introduce new goals.

Sample Mini Routines

Bathroom Mini Routine

1. Pull down pants.
2. Use toilet.
3. (For boys) Put down toilet seat.
4. Flush toilet.
5. Wash hands.
6. Dry hands on towel.

Morning Bedroom Mini Routine

1. Make bed.
2. Remove pajamas.
3. Put on school clothes.
4. Put pajamas away into closet or laundry hamper.

Dressing Mini Routine

1. Remove clothes and place into pile.
2. Put on underpants.
3. Put on pants.
4. Put on shirt.
5. Put on socks.
6. Put on shoes.
7. Put removed clothes into laundry basket.

Morning Bathroom Mini Routine

1. Use toilet.
2. Wash hands.
3. Brush teeth.(See the next routine, Brushing Teeth Mini Mini Routine.)
4. Put away toothbrush and toothpaste.
5. Brush or comb hair.
6. Put away hairbrush.
7. Turn off bathroom light.

Brushing Teeth Mini Mini Routine

1. Get toothbrush and toothpaste.
2. Put toothpaste on toothbrush.
3. Put cap on toothpaste.

4. Brush teeth.

5. Rinse toothbrush.

6. Put toothbrush and toothpaste away.

Breakfast Mini Routine

1. Get out utensils and a plate or bowl.

2. Get out food.

3. Prepare food.

4. Eat food.

5. Clear plate.

6. Clean up food and food prep (eg, pots, pans).

Leaving the House Mini Routine (Young Child)

1. Turn off things that need to be turned off (eg, television set, lights, electronic games).

2. Check to see whether clothes are all on right (especially jacket on, shoes tied, and zippers zipped).

3. Use the bathroom.

4. Grab needed items (eg, backpack, keys).

Leaving the House Mini Routine (Teen)

1. Turn off things that need to be turned off (eg, television set, lights, electronic games).

2. Check to see whether clothes are all on right (especially jacket on, shoes tied, and zippers zipped).

3. Use the bathroom.

4. Grab needed items (eg, backpack, keys, wallet).

5. Lock the door.

Returning Home After School Mini Routine

1. Take off shoes and put away neatly.
2. Hang up jacket.
3. Put backpack away into designated spot.
4. Make or review plan for the afternoon.

Weekend Morning Mini Routine

1. Get out of bed and make bed.
2. Go to the bathroom.
3. Select a quiet activity (from premade list of quiet activities).
4. Get breakfast.
5. Select a quiet activity until family wakes up.

Getting Ready for Bed Mini Routine

1. Take off clothes and put them into a pile.
2. Put on pajamas.
3. Put pile of clothes into laundry hamper.
4. Use the toilet.
5. Wash hands.
6. Brush teeth.
7. Put away toothbrush and toothpaste.
8. Take vitamins.
9. Turn off lights.
10. Get into bed.

Appendix C

Mind Mapping

A **mind map** can help students describe their thoughts by visually organizing information. Major ideas are drawn so that they are connected directly to the main concept, and other ideas branch out from those. For many students, a visual depiction can be easier to understand and memorize. A mind map (such as the one Tatum Elyse Korb created on page 214) conveys the relative importance and relationships between individual ideas and emphasizes the big picture. The best mind maps use mental triggers (eg, colors, connections, and size) to give order to the importance.

The following steps should be considered when creating a mind map:

1. Put the main concept in the center using an image or a title.
2. Create your own images, symbols, and codes to indicate connections and importance.
3. Connect ideas to the main concept using lines that start from the central image. The lines can be made thinner the farther they are from the central image.
4. Each word or image should sit in its own box or on its own line.
5. Use multiple colors throughout the mind map to designate grouping.

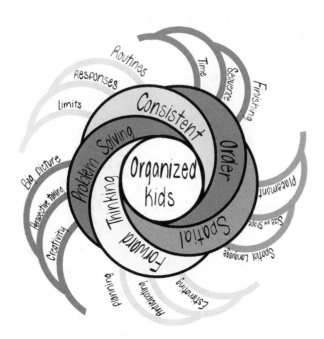

References/Bibliography

References

1. Hartley SL, Barker ET, Seltzer MM, et al. The relative risk and timing of divorce in families of children with an autism spectrum disorder. *J Fam Psychol.* 2010;24(4):449–457

2. Robbers SC, Bartels M, van Beijsterveldt CE, Verhulst FC, Huizink AC, Boomsma DI. Pre-divorce problems in 3-year-olds: a prospective study in boys and girls. *Soc Psychiatry Psychiatr Epidemiol.* 2011;46(4):311–319

3. Swaminathan S, Alexander GR, Boulet S. Delivering a very low birth weight infant and the subsequent risk of divorce or separation. *Matern Child Health J.* 2006;10(6):473–479

4. Bodrova E, Leong DJ. Promoting student's self-regulation in learning. *Educ Dig.* 2005;71(2):54–57

5. Kochanska G, Murray K, Jacques TY, Koenig AL, Vandegeest KA. Inhibitory control in young children and its role in emerging internalization. *Child Dev.* 1996;67(2):490–507

6. Bierman KL, Domitrovich CE, Nix RL, et al. Promoting academic and social-emotional school readiness: the Head Start REDI program. *Child Dev.* 2008;79(6):1802–1817

7. Eslinger PJ, Grattan LM, Geder L. Impact of frontal lobe lesions on rehabilitation and recovery from acute brain injury. *NeuroRehabilitation.* 1995;5(2):161–182

8. Velligan DI, Bow-Thomas CC, Mahurin R, Miller A, Dassori A, Erdely F. Concurrent and predictive validity of the Allen Cognitive Levels Assessment. *Psychiatr Res.* 1998;80(3):287–298

9. Piaget J. *The Construction of Reality in the Child.* Oxford, England: Basic Books; 1954

10. Malloy-Diniz LF, Cardoso-Martins C, Nassif EP, Levy AM, Leite WB, Fuentes D. Planning abilities of children aged 4 years and 9 months to 8 ½ years: effects of age, fluid intelligence and school type on performance in the Tower of London test. *Dement Neuropsychol.* 2008;2(1):26–30

11. Zelazo PD, Reznick JS, Spinazzola J. Representational flexibility and response control in a multistep multilocation search task. *Dev Psychol.* 1998;34(2):203–214

12. Zelazo PD, Müller U. Executive function in typical and atypical development. In: Goswami U, ed. *Handbook of Childhood Cognitive Development.* Oxford, England: Blackwell; 2002:445–469

13. Zelazo PD. The Dimensional Change Card Sort (DCCS): a method of assessing executive function in children. *Nat Protoc.* 2006;1(1):297–301

14. Maughan A, Cicchetti D. Impact of child maltreatment and interadult violence on children's emotion regulation abilities and socioemotional adjustment. *Child Dev.* 2002;73(5):1525–1542

15. O'Connor TG, Rutter M, Beckett C, Keaveney L, Kreppner JM; English and Romanian Adoptees Study Team. The effects of global severe privation on cognitive competence: extension and longitudinal follow-up. *Child Dev.* 2000;71(2):376–390

16. Noble KG, Norman MF, Farah MJ. Neurocognitive correlates of socioeconomic status in kindergarten children. *Dev Sci.* 2005;8(1):74–87

17. Bos KJ, Fox N, Zeanah CH, Nelson CA III. Effects of early psychosocial deprivation on the development of memory and executive function. *Front Behav Neurosci.* 2009;3:16

18. Colvert E, Rutter M, Kreppner J, et al. Do theory of mind and executive function deficits underlie the adverse outcomes associated with profound early deprivation? Findings from the English and Romanian Adoptees Study. *J Abnorm Child Psychol.* 2008;36(7):1057–1068

19. Feldman R. The development of regulatory functions from birth to 5 years: insights from premature infants. *Child Dev.* 2009;80(2):544–561

20. Luciana M, Lindeke L, Georgieff M, Mills M, Nelson CA. Neurobehavioral evidence for working-memory deficits in school-aged children with histories of prematurity. *Dev Med Child Neurol.* 1999;41(8):521–533

21. Lewis EE, Dozier M, Ackerman J, Sepulveda-Kozakowski S. The effect of placement instability on adopted children's inhibitory control abilities and oppositional behavior. *Dev Psychol.* 2007;43(6):1415–1427

22. Barkley RA. The executive functions and self-regulation: an evolutionary neuropsychological perspective. *Neuropsychol Rev.* 2001;11(1):1–29

23. Dunbar RI, Shultz S. Evolution in the social brain. *Science.* 2007;317(5843):1344–1347

24. Blair C, Razza RP. Relating effortful control, executive function, and false belief understanding to emerging math and literacy ability in kindergarten. *Child Dev.* 2007;78(2):647–663

25. Espy K, McDiarmid MD, Cwik MF, Meade Stalets M, Hamby A. The contribution of executive functions to emergent mathematic skills in preschool children. In: *Developmental Cognitive Neuroscience Laboratory - Faculty and Staff Publications.* Lincoln, NE: University of Nebraska–Lincoln. DCNL publication 7

26. Howse R, Calkins S, Anastopoulos A, Keane S, Shelton T. Regulatory contributors to children's kindergarten achievement. *Early Educ Dev.* 2003;14(1):101–120

27. Haith MM, Hazan C, Goodman GS. Expectation and anticipation of dynamic visual events by 3.5-month-old babies. *Child Dev.* 1988;59(2):467–479

28. McColgan KL, McCormack T. Searching and planning: young children's reasoning about past and future event sequences. *Child Dev.* 2008;79(5):1477–1497

29. Mischel W. *Advances in Experimental Social Psychology.* New York, NY: Academic Press; 1974:249–292. Berkowitz L, ed. *Processes in Delay of Gratification*; vol 7

30. Hetland L. Learning to make music enhances spatial reasoning. *J Aesthetic Educ.* 2000;34(3/4):179–238

31. Costa-Giomi E. The effects of three years of piano instruction on children's cognitive development. *J Res Music Educ.* 1999;47(3):198–212

32. Evans DE, Whipp P, Lay SB. Knowledge representation and pattern recognition skills of elite adult and youth soccer players. *Int J Perform Anal Sport.* 2012;12(1):208–221

33. Faubert J. Professional athletes have extraordinary skills for rapidly learning complex and neutral dynamic visual scenes. *Sci Rep.* 2013;3(1):1154

34. Voss MW, Kramer AF, Basak C, Prakash RS, Roberts B. Are expert athletes "expert" in the cognitive laboratory? A meta-analytic review of cognition and sport expertise. *Appl Cogn Psychol.* 2010;24(6):812–826

35. Mann DT, Williams AM, Ward P, Janelle CM. Perceptual-cognitive expertise in sport: a meta-analysis. *J Sport Exerc Psychol.* 2007;29(4):457–478

36. American Academy of Pediatrics. Lack of sleep is associated with increased risk of injury in adolescent athletes. American Academy of Pediatrics National Conference & Exhibition; October 21, 2012; New Orleans, LA

37. Christensen DL, Baio J, Braun KV, et al. Prevalence and characteristics of autism spectrum disorder among children aged 8 years — Autism and Developmental Disabilities Monitoring Network, 11 sites, United States, 2012. *MMWR Surveill Summ.* 2016;65(3):1–23

38. Baron-Cohen S. *Mindblindness: An Essay on Autism and Theory of Mind.* Cambridge, MA: MIT; 1995

39. Zilbovicius M, Garreau B, Samson Y, et al. Delayed maturation of the frontal cortex in childhood autism. *Am J Psychiatry.* 1995;152(2):248–252

40. Ozonoff S, Cook I, Coon H, et al. Performance on Cambridge Neuropsychological Test Automated Battery subtests sensitive to frontal lobe function in people with autistic disorder: evidence from the Collaborative Programs of Excellence in Autism network. *J Autism Dev Disord.* 2004;34(2):139–150

41. Happé F, Booth R, Charlton R, Hughes C. Executive function deficits in autism spectrum disorders and attention-deficit/hyperactivity disorder: examining profiles across domains and ages. *Brain Cogn.* 2006;61(1):25–39

42. Pennington BF, Ozonoff S. Executive functions and developmental psychopathology. *J Child Psychol Psychiatry.* 1996;37(1):51–87

43. Marco EJ, Hinkley LBN, Hill SS, Nagarajan SS. Sensory processing in autism: a review of neurophysiologic findings. *Pediatr Res.* 2011;69(5, pt 2):48R–54R

44. Mesibov GB, Shea V, Schopler E. *The TEACCH Approach to Autism Spectrum Disorders.* New York, NY: Springer; 2005

45. Polanczyk G, de Lima MS, Horta BL, Biederman J, Rohde LA. The worldwide prevalence of ADHD: a systematic review and metaregression analysis. *Am J Psychiatry.* 2007;164(6):942–948

46. Thomas R, Sanders S, Doust J, Beller E, Glasziou P. Prevalence of attention-deficit/hyperactivity disorder: a systematic review and meta-analysis. *Pediatrics*. 2015;135(4):e994–e1001

47. Russell B. *A Clinician's Manual for Assessment and Parent Training*. New York, NY: Guilford; 1997

48. Arnsten AF. Toward a new understanding of attention-deficit hyperactivity disorder pathophysiology: an important role for prefrontal cortex dysfunction. *CNS Drugs*. 2009;23(1)(suppl 1):33–41

49. Hosenbocus S, Chahal R. A review of executive function deficits and pharmacological management in children and adolescents. *J Can Acad Child Adolesc Psychiatry*. 2012;21(3):223–229

50. Snyder AM, Maruff P, Pietrzak RH, Cromer JR, Snyder PJ. Effect of treatment with stimulant medication on nonverbal executive function and visuomotor speed in children with attention deficit/hyperactivity disorder (ADHD). *Child Neuropsychol*. 2008;14(3):211–226

51. Green T, Weinberger R, Diamond A, et al. The effect of methylphenidate on prefrontal cognitive functioning, inattention, and hyperactivity in velocardiofacial syndrome. *J Child Adolesc Psychopharmacol*. 2011;21(6):589–595

Bibliography

Addis DR, Wong AT, Schacter DL. Age-related changes in the episodic simulation of future events. *Psychol Sci*. 2008;19(1):33–41

Allen CK, Allen RE. Cognitive disabilities: measuring the social consequences of mental disorders. *J Clin Psychiatry*. 1987;48(5):185–190

Anderson SW, Bechara A, Damasio H, Tranel D, Damasio AR. Impairment of social and moral behavior related to early damage in human prefrontal cortex. *Nat Neurosci*. 1999;2(11):1032–1037

Baum CM, Connor LT, Morrison T, Hahn M, Dromerick AW, Edwards DF. Reliability, validity, and clinical utility of the Executive Function Performance Test: a measure of executive function in a sample of people with stroke. *Am J Occup Ther*. 2008;62(4):446–455

Blakemore SJ, Frith U. *The Learning Brain: Lessons for Education*. Oxford, England: Blackwell; 2005

Bloomquist ML. *Skills Training for Children With Behavior Problems: A Parent and Practitioner Guidebook*. Rev ed. New York, NY: Guilford; 2006

Busby J, Suddendorf T. Recalling yesterday and predicting tomorrow. *Cogn Dev.* 2005;20(3):362–272

Byrnes JP. *Minds, Brains, and Learning: Understanding the Psychological and Educational Relevance of Neuroscientific Research*. New York, NY: Guilford; 2001

Carper RA, Courchesne E. Localized enlargement of the frontal cortex in early autism. *Biol Psychiatry.* 2005;57(2):126–133

Dahl RE. Adolescent brain development: a period of vulnerabilities and opportunities. Keynote address. *Ann N Y Acad Sci.* 2004;1021(1):1–22

D'Argembeau A, Van der Linden M. Phenomenal characteristics associated with projecting oneself back into the past and forward into the future: influence of valence and temporal distance. *Conscious Cogn.* 2004;13(4):844–858

Diamond A. Normal development of prefrontal cortex from birth to young adulthood: cognitive functions, anatomy, and biochemistry. In: Stuss DT, Knight RT, eds. *Principles of Frontal Lobe Function*. London, England: Oxford University; 2002:466–503

Dowsett SM, Livesey DJ. The development of inhibitory control in preschool children: effects of "executive skills" training. *Dev Psychobiol.* 2000;36(2):161–174

Fabricius WV. The development of forward search planning in preschoolers. *Child Dev.* 1988;59(6):1473–1488

Ferber R. *Solve Your Child's Sleep Problems*. New York, NY: Simon & Schuster; 1986

Fuster JM. Frontal lobe and cognitive development. *J Neurocytol.* 2002;31(3–5):373–385

Fuster JM. *The Prefrontal Cortex*. New York, NY: Raven; 1980

Gillam RB, Crofford JA, Gale MA, Hoffman LM. Language change following computer-assisted language instruction with Fast ForWord or Laureate Learning Systems software. *Am J Speech Lang Pathol.* 2001;10(3):231–247

Greene R. *The Explosive Child: A New Approach for Understanding and Parenting Easily Frustrated, Chronically Inflexible Children*. New York, NY: HarperCollins; 2009

Hassabis D, Kumaran D, Vann SD, Maguire EA. Patients with hippocampal amnesia cannot imagine new experiences. *Proc Natl Acad Sci USA.* 2007;104(5):1726–1731

Hill EL. Evaluating the theory of executive dysfunction in autism. *Dev Rev.* 2004;24(2):189–233

Hook PE, Macaruso P, Jones S. Efficacy of Fast ForWord training on facilitating acquisition of reading skills by children with reading difficulties—a longitudinal study. *Ann Dyslexia.* 2001;51(1):73–96

Huttenlocher P. *Neural Plasticity: The Effects of Environment on the Development of the Cerebral Cortex.* Cambridge, MA: Harvard University; 2002

Kaller CP, Rahm B, Spreer J, Mader I, Unterrainer JM. Thinking around the corner: the development of planning abilities. *Brain Cogn.* 2008;67(3):360–370

Klingberg T, Fernell E, Olesen PJ, et al. Computerized training of working memory in children with ADHD—a randomized, controlled trial. *J Am Acad Child Adolesc Psychiatry.* 2005;44(2):177–186

Magnée JCM, de Gelder B, van Engeland H, Kemmer C. Audiovisual speech integration in pervasive developmental disorder: evidence from event-related potentials. *J Child Psychol Psychiatry.* 2008;49(9):995–1000

Marzano R, Pickering D, Pollock J. *Classroom Instruction That Works.* Alexandria, VA: Association for Supervision and Curriculum Development; 2001

Mischel W, Ebbesen EB, Zeiss AR. Cognitive and attentional mechanisms in delay of gratification. *J Pers Soc Psychol.* 1972;21(2):204–218

Olesen PJ, Westerberg H, Klingberg T. Increased prefrontal and parietal activity after training of working memory. *Nat Neurosci.* 2004;7(1):75–79

Prencipe A, Zelazo PD. Development of affective decision making for self and other: evidence for the integration of first- and third-person perspectives. *Psychol Sci.* 2005;16(7):501–505

Price BH, Daffner KR, Stowe RM, Mesulam MM. The comportmental learning disabilities of early frontal lobe damage. *Brain.* 1990;113(pt 5):1383–1393

Royall DR, Lauterbach EC, Cummings JL, et al. Executive control function: a review of its promise and challenges for clinical research. A report from the Committee on Research of the American Neuropsychiatric Association. *J Neuropsychiatry Clin Neurosci.* 2002;14(4):377–405

Rueda MR, Rothbart MK, McCandliss BD, Saccomanno L, Posner MI. Training, maturation, and genetic influences on the development of executive attention. *Proc Natl Acad Sci USA.* 2005;102(41):14931–14936

Russo N, Nicol T, Trommer B, Zecker S, Kraus N. Brainstem transcription of speech is disrupted in children with autism spectrum disorders. *Dev Sci.* 2009;12(4):557–567

Russo NM, Skoe E, Trommer B, et al. Deficient brainstem encoding of pitch in children with autism spectrum disorders. *Clin Neurophysiol.* 2008;119(8):1720–1731

Sanchez-Marin FJ, Padilla-Medina JA. A psychophysical test of the visual pathway of children with autism. *J Autism Dev Disord.* 2008;38(7):1270–1277

Schultz RT. Developmental deficits in social perception in autism: the role of the amygdala and fusiform face area. *Int J Dev Neurosci.* 2005;23(2–3):125–141

Séguin JR, Zelazo PD. Executive function in early physical aggression. In: Tremblay RE, Hartup WW, Archer J, eds. *Developmental Origins of Aggression.* New York, NY: Guilford; 2005:307–329

Smaers JB, Steele J, Case CR, Cowper A, Amunts K, Zilles K. Primate prefrontal cortex evolution: human brains are the extreme of a lateralized ape trend. *Brain Behav Evol.* 2011;77(2):67–78

Suddendorf T, Nielsen M, von Gehlen R. Children's capacity to remember a novel problem and to secure its future solution. *Dev Sci.* 2011;14(1):26–33

Temple E, Deutsch GK, Poldrack RA, et al. Neural deficits in children with dyslexia ameliorated by behavioral remediation: evidence from functional MRI. *Proc Natl Acad Sci USA.* 2003;100(5):2860–2865

Tremblay RE, Nagin DS, Séguin JR, et al. Physical aggression during early childhood: trajectories and predictors. *Pediatrics.* 2004;114(1):e43–e50

Westerberg H, Hirvikoski T, Forssberg H, Klingberg T. Visuo-spatial working memory span: a sensitive measure of cognitive deficits in children with ADHD. *Child Neuropsychol.* 2004;10(3):155–161

Index